DATE DUE

JUN 1 1 1985			
JUN 1 9 1985			
DEC 1 5 1988			
DEC 0 3 1991			
GAYLORD			PRINTED IN U.S.A.

60 UNBEATEN PATHS
AN UNUSUAL GUIDE TO THE
UNUSUAL IN THE NORTHWEST

Photography by

BOB and IRA SPRING

Text by

BYRON FISH

Maps by Helen Sherman

Superior PUBLISHING COMPANY

708 SIXTH AVE. NORTH, SEATTLE, WASH.

Cover photo: A road in the Steens Mountains
Page 2: Sand dunes in Christmas Valley

(The article about Hell's Canyon, pages 134-136, first appeared
in Ford Times and is reprinted by permission).

CONTENTS

Page

FOREWORD: *What Are Unbeaten Paths?* 7

CAPE ALAVA—*Where Settlers Decided They Were Too Far West* 11

BEACHCOMBING—*The Ocean Delivers Keen Junk* 14

SHIPWRECKS—*Lloyds of London Hated This Coast* 20

LIGHTHOUSES—*They Decorate the Coasts* 23

BOUNDARY MARKERS—*Two Parties on the 49th Came Out Parallel* 24

A RARE PLANT—*Tweedy Also Surveyed Flowers* 26

RHODODENDRONS—*They Follow the Ancestral Pattern* 28

ELK—*They Go Under an Alias* 31

BIRD REFUGES—*You Can Count People in Them* 32

MIMA MOUNDS—*A Mysterious Case of Hives* 35

FORT VANCOUVER—*Once Capital of the Pacific Northwest* 36

MT. ADAMS LAVA FIELDS—*A Hot Show Went on Here, Too* 38

THE LONGEST LOGGING FLUME—
It's Owned by the "Lassie Lumber Co." 40

BARLOW TOLL ROAD—*It Was Better Than Drowning* 42

NACHES PASS WAGON ROAD—*Drowning Might Have Been Better* 44

COLUMBIA GORGE WATERFALLS—*Streams That Don't Meander* 46

HORSETHIEF LAKE—*The Region's First Shopping Center* 48

FORT SIMCOE—*The Indians Let You Visit It* 53

GINGKO PETRIFIED FOREST—*Sustained Yield Program Takes Time* 54

MOSES COULEE—*Moses Never Reached the Promised Land* 56

DRY FALLS—*It Didn't Stay in One Place* 60

BLUE LAKE RHINO—*A Bad Day in Black Rocks* 62

HIDDEN COULEES—*Places to Carry Snakebite Kits* 64

POTHOLES LAKES—*You Can Have an Island to Yourself* 69

A VERY MEAN INDIAN 70

ROCKWALLED MYSTERIES 71

BATTLE BUTTE—*A Peaceful Place* 72

MARYHILL AND STONEHENGE—*What Was In Sam Hill's Idea Anyway?* 74

PALOUSE FALLS—*It Kept Its Coulee* 76

MARMES MAN—*The Country's Oldest Resident* 78

WHITMAN MISSION—*The Real Massacre Was of Indians* 81

WASHINGTON GHOST TOWNS—*Gone With the Timber* 82

OREGON GHOST TOWNS—*Or, On to the Next Gold Strike* 85

IDAHO GHOST TOWNS—*Too Much for the Earps or Calamity Jane* 86

SHANIKO, OREGON—*It sure Missed the Train* 88

PAINTED HILLS—*In Strawberry, Vanilla and Chocolate* 91

BLUE BUCKET OF GOLD—*Did It Ever Exist?* 92

ROCKHOUND'S PARADISE—*Prineville Stakes the Claim* 94

ARROWHEADS—*Find Them and You'll Get the Point* 96

STEIN'S PILLAR—*A Ridiculous Rock* 97

SHERAR'S BRIDGE—*Travelers Bawled at the Tolls* 98

PICTURE GORGE—*Kilroy and Others Were Here* 100

SMITH ROCKS—*A Swatch of Peaks Attract Mountaineers* 102

LAVA FLOW AREA—*Newberry's Walls Were Like Jericho's* 104

McKENZIE PASS—*Where the Blacktop Ran Amok* 108

FORT ROCK—*Lava and Water Don't Mix* 110

CHRISTMAS VALLEY—*Real Estate Subject to a Sandy Clause* 113

GLASS BUTTES—*So Far They Are Unrecycled* 115

STEENS MOUNTAINS—*Another of Oregon's Big Faults* 116

MALHEUR WILDLIFE REFUGE—*Oregon's Largest Poultry Yard* 122

HART MOUNTAIN—*Where the Pelican and the Antelope Play* 124

COVERED CROSSINGS—*Lane County's Bridge Game* 126

MULLAN ROAD—*It Was U.S. Interterritorial No. 1* 129

CATALDO MISSION—*More Than Idaho's Oldest Building* 131

ST. JOE RIVER—*It Never Knew When It Was Licked* 132

HELL'S CANYON—*The Colorado's Grand Canyon is Shallower* 134

HOMESTEADS IN THE WILDERNESS 138

IN PRAISE OF PAINT SPRAY-CANS 140

SUPPLEMENTARY READING—*For Special Interests* 142

FOREWORD
What Are Unbeaten Paths?

What constitutes an "unbeaten path" to go with the title of this book is a question that can be argued from several viewpoints. Many of the places reviewed are standards on the tourist trail, long marked in red ink on highway maps as sites of interest.

How many motorists, though, actually stop to see them? Old Fort Vancouver and its apple tree (pages 36-37) are within sight of Interstate 5 as it goes through Vancouver, Wash., but northbound vacationers have told their relatives they will arrive in Seattle by 5 p.m., and southbound motorists are in a hurry to cross the bridge into Oregon where they can buy cheaper cigarettes, with no sales tax, either.

Times and traffic patterns change with new highways. Jackson Courthouse, and Mima Mounds (page 34) on old Highway 99 are now bypassed and who leaves the freeway to take them in now? Next time, maybe.

Other places we have included are either unpublicized or they are far enough off pavement that only the more curious and adventuresome will go looking for them. They are reached by dirt roads that a driver of an ordinary passenger car will sweat out before he thankfully emerges on blacktop again.

Some are faint foot trails made more interesting by the fact that hikers should wear heavy boots and not step on rattlesnakes. Some have no trails at all, you just climb around where fancy dictates.

In general, this book has two themes, although the first is more an arbitrary action than a theme.

The author and the photographers have covered the Pacific Northwest territory to-

Farm in Moses Coulee

gether for more than 20 years. We have collaborated on half a dozen Superior Publishing Company books about one section or another (or Alaska).

We thought it was time for a recapitulation. What we present here are the offbeat spots that never made other books; new areas we have discovered meanwhile (it's a big country) and those old ones that we fully believe are worth a second look.

Part of the arbitrary decision was the conclusion that only in a few cases does anyone need point-to-point instructions on how to get to these destinations. Federal, state, county and Forest Service roads are numbered and they are all on maps readily obtained at service stations or other sources. This book therefore makes no pretense of being a comprehensive guide unless some special instructions are needed in the immediate area.

For the same reason, it does not try to pinpoint where to find thunder eggs, emperor geese, arrowheads, shipwrecks or ghost towns. Anyone interested in these subjects will have studied far more detailed reference books. This one merely mentions the areas that knowledgeable hobbyists already know are productive. They may hate us for pointing it out to more people.

If there is really a theme aside from the author-photographer choice of favorite subjects, it is that on the second (or third or fourth) round, things do begin to tie together, geologically and in the history of mankind.

The deep lava beds of Grand Coulee and those of the huge face of Abert Rim or the Steens Mountains in southern Oregon were probably laid down in the same epoch and were exposed by different means, one by erosion and the other by faulting.

Everyone has heard of Mt. Mazama, the volcano that blew up and left Crater Lake cradled in its remaining foundations. The role played by an equally huge volcano, Mt. Newberry, southwest of Bend, Oregon, is only now being brought to light. It was a hot center until recent times.

This is no geology book either, but in the grouping of subjects we have tried to put them together so that a very ancient trail, from prehistoric times to within memory of human inhabitants, can be traced in eruptions and lava flows.

The Columbia Basin and Oregon lava flows, the rising of the Cascade Mountains and the new eruptions at Mt. Adams, McKenzie Pass, Lava Butte and Christmas Valley

Gardner Cave, northeast Washington

Heceta lighthouse, Oregon coast

were all "current events" at one time and they formed the Pacific Northwest.

A few other subjects are not treated entirely geographically. You will not be visiting the Barlow Toll Road and the Naches Pass wagon road on the same road map trip, but both were constructed by the prodigious efforts of first settlers in the region, in the attempt to help emigrants cross the barriers of the Cascade Range. They are equally part of that story.

Then there is the decision of what to put in, what to leave out. In a region so rich with choices, sometimes it comes down to stubborn arguments between the writer and the photographers.

There is nothing photogenic, for example, about the Mean Indian's grave on page 70. Cameramen like to take something more scenic. Writers are fascinated by such legends and the aura of mystery that goes with them. This page appears only at the insistence of the author whose wife, a one-time resident of the area, tipped him off to the story. She also appears in the photo.

Within the area covered, as many worthwhile places have been left out as have been put in. There just isn't room for them all, and some boundaries had to be drawn. The caves described, for example, are all lava tubes, yet both Washington and Oregon have the type formed by sedimentary erosion, with stalactites and stalagmites from calcium carbonate deposits dripped from the ceiling.

One such cave is in southwest Oregon, long commercially exploited. The other is Gardner Cave, in a Washington State park little visited because it is so far up in the northeast corner of the state.

We did not get around to the salmon run and fish hatcheries, well worth pages in themselves. On the other hand, neither was there room for more than passing mention of the sights in Moses Coulee (pages 56-59) and the "most photographed lighthouse" (pages 22-23 and here).

Now you know what we mean by "unbeaten paths." We hope you will enjoy them by reading or in person. In following these roads, you can come upon many more such places on your own.

CAPE ALAVA AND SMUGGLERS' COVE
Where Settlers Decided They Were Too Far West

America's tide of migration rippled across the continent to its farthest coast along the Olympic Peninsula, and there it acted as all high tides do. One wave went slightly beyond the rest and receded, leaving only a damp spot on the beach.

Fifteen miles south of Cape Flattery, the sharp tip at the entrance to the Strait of Juan de Fuca, the coastline bulges mildly as Cape Alava, the farthest west point in the 48 joined-together states.

Just inland from it is Lake Ozette. Homesteaders of Scandinavian descent arrived there in the 1890's, surrounding the lake with homes, school, church and post office. One, Lars K. Ahlstrom, went on to start a ranch in the forest clearing, where he lived for 58 years as "the farthest west resident in the continental United States."

Except for Ahlstrom, the frontier line soon fell back. Many homesteaders took off for Alaska gold rushes. The rest melted away over the next two decades. Ozette was reached only by trail, 25 miles, or by boat and trail from Cape Alava. "Outside" people were not walking by then, they were running around in automobiles.

Before a road reached Ozette there was nobody left, not even the original inhabitants of the village at the Cape. A smallpox epidemic struck and the last of the Ozette Indians moved away or had died by 1925. Their houses slowly collapsed and were covered by a nearly impenetrable jungle.

Logging reached the east side of the lake and a road ended at the north end, where a small resort was started with no great success. Some years ago the forested strip between lake and ocean was taken into the Olympic National Park's detached seacoast preserve, thus insuring against a return migration wave of real estate developers.

The three-mile trail from lake to seashore, plus a mile north to the cape, was popular with those who found out Alava was as far west as they could go at high tide. They could beat even that record at low tide when a sandspit connected the cape to Indian Island, a tall hump a couple of hundred yards out, with a grove of trees on its flat top. It was used as a Coast Guard observatory during the Second World War.

Rocks of "Cannonball Island"

(Left page) Petroglyph at Ozette village

11

The bark "Austria" crashed here in 1887.

A Midwestern newspaperman was once so intrigued by the idea of becoming the Most-Farwestern correspondent he took a taxi all the way from Port Angeles to Lake Ozette. He had to walk the last four miles, of course, and after that taxi bill, probably back to Port Angeles.

Hikers stopped midway on the trail to chat with Ahlstrom, and at the beach they peered curiously into the brush at the remnants of the Indian village. Then in the late 1960's archeologists from the state universities became interested in the site. Their curiosity was mild at first, but as work progressed they struck it rich.

While it was found that Indians had lived on the cape for centuries, fishing and going to sea on whale hunts, it was not the great antiquity of the village that made it so interesting. In a climate that in a few years rots timber, let alone more fragile articles, a clay slide had buried and almost hermetically sealed houses and their contents, preserving a culture uninfluenced by white explorers.

The Cape Alava trail never before saw so much pedestrian traffic. Each summer since, digging crews and sidewalk superintendents have been coming and going.

Except for that, it is a wild stretch of coast with jagged reefs offshore. The bark "Austria" dropped anchor here in 1887 but not on purpose. It smashed on the reefs and at low water the anchor can be seen rusting on the beach.

A little farther south, opposite the end of Lake Ozette, a Norwegian skipper in 1903 mistook a beach cabin light for the Tatoosh lighthouse at Cape Flattery and turned inward. Two of the crew of 20 survived and the rest are buried at the Norwegian Memorial there.

A lightship is anchored at sea west of the reefs and Cape Alava to give ships the "no-right-turn" signal until they get to Cape Flattery. We watched its blinker one night while camped on Indian Island—feeling farthest west except for that floating lighthouse out beyond us.

The round rocks at the base of Indian

Island, which have given it also the name of "Cannonball Island," are a curiosity that geologists still argue about. One theory is that they are so old they were worn into that shape by the rolling action of ancient seas, imbedded later and then cast loose by erosion. Another theory is that they are "concretions," but nobody knows why a concretion should assume a perfectly round form.

SMUGGLERS' COVE

North of Cape Alava, near Flattery, is one of those inlets always described as a "smugglers' cove." Every hidden entrance on a coastline close to Canada gathered its own folklore about Prohibition days when rumrunners brought liquor across the border.

One might wonder why rumrunners put into hiding places so far from their customers or why revenue cutter agents, who also knew their coastlines, were so often baffled in their pursuit of illicit traffic that suddenly vanished. The legends give an aura of romance, though, to narrow clefts and to any

shack ever built on an inside beach by the most innocent fisherman or hermit.

This one yawns at the hiker's feet on a short trail to the point overlooking Cape Flattery and Tatoosh Island. It may or may not have been used as a hide-out but it looks up to its role, which is what counts.

There is a fascination about all of nature's hidden doorways, whether they lead in from the sea or over high mountain passes. Caves and cracks in the earth (discussed elsewhere in this book) are in the same category. They afford a peek, however slight, at the earth's mysterious underpinnings.

A not-readily-apparent cleft in the rocks leading from one coulee to another invites exploration. Every box canyon conjures a vision of a lost world on the other side, or if an old trail or road runs through it, the belief that it at least once must have been the scene of an ambush.

More than one of these sea inlets may have been used for that purpose, too. The Haidas ranged the coast in their war canoes, raiding the camps of other tribes and carrying away slaves.

Entrance to "Smugglers' Cove."

BEACHCOMBING
The Ocean Delivers Keen Junk

Beaches are for combing, an all-season sport with innumerable interpretations of what constitutes the score. The most obvious treasures are semi-precious stones, delicate shells, driftwood to decorate gardens or to preserve as "sculpture," and fuel for beach-fires.

Discoveries do not have to be lugged away. Some are too big or too imbedded in the sand, besides being useless. However, the keel of a wrecked ship, a crate on which Japanese characters are stencilled or a large chunk of cork give satisfaction just in finding them. They stimulate the imagination—how did they arrive there?

Nothing seems impossible in the inventory of what the sea can cast up. In observing that fact while walking a wild beach, the Walter Mitty in all of us becomes Robinson Crusoe. We don't have to salvage this barrel or that piece of iron, but now if we were castaways . . .

Residents along Pacific beaches put to good use the supplies brought in by the tide. Many a cabin has been built primarily from dimension lumber delivered free in the front yard or not far from it. It may have come from a storm-stricken barge that got away from its towboat, or from dunnage, the planks and other timbers used to support cargo and thrown overboard afterwards.

Camping on the Washington coast, we have quickly erected a shelter from beams and boards, with a large log as the backwall and a rainproof roof thatched with dry sea-weed. In the Crusoe role, we found not only a corked, empty flask but a quarter-bottle of ink for writing the message to put in it. Just wait and the tide brings you everything.

Top prizes are the glass floats from fishing nets. They drift over from the Orient, carried by the Japan Current. They are of Russian, Japanese or Korean manufacture and some-times are marked so the source can be iden-

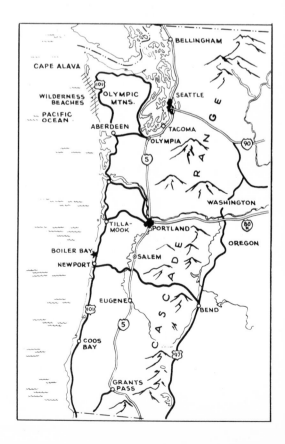

Storm waves whip up foam that hides glass floats.

tified. The commonest sizes are three to six inches in diameter but occasionally they run to 18 inches or more.

Most of the spheres are greenish but they may be clear, amber, reddish or otherwise tinted. How long they were afloat is anyone's guess. It could have been as little as six or seven months but a year is more likely.

Those in earnest about hunting floats head for the beach right after a winter storm to catch new arrivals, if any. By summer the strands will have been well searched but a chance remains of finding a glass ball or a tubular-shaped float wedged among the driftwood tossed high by big waves on an incoming tide.

Beachcombers have a somewhat more exciting time on the Washington coast than they do in Oregon. Oregon's beaches are readily accessible from the highway but less than a fifth of Washington's coast is on a through route. The rest of the beaches are either stretched along lengthy dead-end roads or are reached by trail, which reduces the number of dilettantes.

Another factor in Washington's favor is simply that the main ocean current runs south, thus giving the northern beaches first crack at the good stuff.

The beaches vary from hard-packed sand that motorists can drive on for many miles, as on the North Beach Peninsula (southwestern Washington) to walled-off stretches of a mile or so. Headlands scallop the coast, with passage around them only at low tide so each curving beach between jutting points is a separate entity. South of La Push they are named "First Beach," "Second Beach" and "Third Beach." They continue, but at that point the tide must have come in and turned back whoever was numbering them.

The 15 miles from Third Beach to the Hoh River (where a dirt road leads back to U.S. 101) is a two-day hike, climbing headlands or waiting to go around them on an ebb tide. The 19 miles north from La Push to Lake Ozette could be done a little quicker but only if no time is allotted to enjoy it.

Winter storm at Ruby Beach, with Abbey Island off-shore.

A boiler came by barge to Third Beach and was muscled up this trail. One belief is that it was used in an early-century attempt to strike oil, but others say it was for steam logging.

A steamship was wrecked here before Oregonians
had named all their bays and coves. This one became,
simply enough, Boiler Bay.

Driftwood at Second Beach, Olympic National Park
Ocean Strip. The framed rock is one of the Quillayute
Needles.

SHIPWRECKS
Lloyds of London Hated This Coast

The way for a ship to add lore to a seacoast and, in many cases, gain immortality for itself, is to end its days by wrecking on the shore. Shipowners and mariners do not equate such finales with a successful voyage, but the public does.

Ships that plod on their way for a working lifetime without undue incident generally go to the boneyard the same way. Those that suffer spectacular misfortune have given their names to reefs and coves, and if they happen to hit a beach frequented by people, their remains automatically become their monument.

An equally effective path to fame is to sink offshore in water not so deep but what it is a challenge to divers, especially if there is a story afloat that the ship carried riches of some sort. The treasure is not really necessary as long as the ship carried the rumor.

The Washington-Oregon coast cannot compete with Florida in that respect, because everything that ever sunk off Florida was reputed to be a Spanish treasure ship. Furthermore, they sank in droves, whole fleets that according to legend were laden with gold for Spain when they were driven ashore by a typhoon.

The first ships along the Northwest coast were explorers just snooping. The next ones were traders, but what they had on board were trinkets they hoped to swap with the Indians for furs. If they got wrecked inbound the stuff would not be much good today, and if they wrecked outbound, the same could be said of the furs.

Today's beach-wanderer might as well face it, he is not about to find doubloons or anything of more than historical value if he comes across remnants of a shipwreck. There have been plenty of them, though.

A number of seacoasts in the world claim to be "the grave-yard of ships," but for the relatively short time it has been a contender, the mouth of the Columbia River rates with the best. Well over 100 vessels failed to make the bar and have been scattered up the beach, mostly to the north.

Their bones as timbers or bits of metal can be found strewn from south of the Columbia River to Cape Flattery, another treacherous place where ships have missed the turn into the Strait of Juan de Fuca.

The least glamorous of all shipwrecks on the beach today is at Ocean Shores, just north of Grays Harbor. The old Catala, having ended a seagoing career, was used as a floating hotel during the Seattle World Fair of 1962. Then it was towed to Ocean Shores to perform the same duty.

A storm broke it loose, tossed it around a point and jammed it into the sand forevermore. No Coast Guard rescue, no lives lost, but it does sit there rather dramatically, looking like a shipwreck and preserving its name.

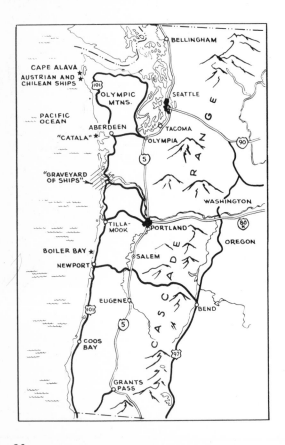

The Catala won more fame as a shipwreck than it did as a floating hotel.

LIGHTHOUSES
They Decorate the Coast

Some people like to visit cathedrals, some like to prowl through castles and others prefer lighthouses as a form of architecture. Something all these structures have in common is a long history and that they were built to last.

Lighthouses came into being more than 2,000 years ago and ran on wood or coal beacon fires, or candles, until the middle of the 18th century, when oil came into use. Next it was electricity, but the change in operation methods still goes on. Lighthouse keepers become fewer each year as the stations are automated and monitored by radio.

It makes lighthouse lovers sad. They like to think humans are inside the buildings. Part of their fascination is with the life—real or imaginary—of the keepers. Being at least a part-time hermit sounds more attractive each year of the 20th Century, and to get paid for it too . . .

Some of the oldest structures in Washington and Oregon are lighthouses. The first one was erected on Cape Disappointment, at the mouth of the Columbia, in 1856.

Many construction dates are hard to pin down because the original was rebuilt later. Dungeness, on the Strait of Juan De Fuca, has had a light since 1857 but apparently the present site goes back only to 1927. The Coast Guard, which took over these navigation aids in 1939, gives both dates for "New Dungeness."

The Tatoosh Island station off Cape Flattery has been in operation since 1857 and so has Umpqua, although it was rebuilt in 1894. Ediz Hook is more than a century old—1865—and Oregon's Cape Blanco lighthouse, standing highest above the sea at 245 feet, was built in 1870.

The favorites among photographers are the white conical towers. They look like a lighthouse should. The Oregon coast is best supplied with these, including the tallest one, Yaquina Head, 93 feet, which puts the light 162 feet above the sea. However, Cape Blanco and Umpqua are the only ones still run by men who live at the station.

Perhaps the two most photographed lighthouses are 56-foot Heceta Head in Oregon, built in 1894, and Washington's North Head, a 65-foot tower dating to 1898. Both stand high above the sea on imposing cliffs.

Washington has more lighthouses, because of its inland channels and islands. These are smaller, from 20 to 46 feet high, and generally octagonal instead of round. Those at Point Wilson, Point No Point, West Point, Alki and Point Robinson on Maury Island were built between 1879 and 1887, although they all were revised during the early part of the century. So far, they are manned.

The two lightships are anchored too far out for pictures or visiting but they can be seen on clear days. The entrance to the Columbia River has been guarded by a ship since 1892. The Umatilla, at a reef of the same name a few miles south of Flattery, has been on duty since 1898.

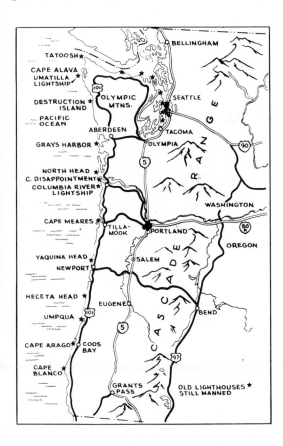

(Opposite) North Head lighthouse

BOUNDARY MARKERS
Two Parties on the 49th Came Out Parallel

After the War of 1812 was over, Britain and the United States spent four years trying to figure out who won it. They came to no definite conclusion and finally signed an "as-you-were" treaty in 1818. The international boundary still ran along the 49th Parallel from Lake of the Woods west and was left hanging at the Continental Divide.

The next round of the argument was whether it ran south from there. In the 1840's, both sides were claiming Oregon Territory. By hollering for everything north to Russian Alaska, the United States got Britain to compromise along the old line—the 49th Parallel.

That was in 1846. Ten years later they concluded they ought to find out where the 49th Parallel was. Unlike most international borders based on topography or ethnic groups, this new one was entirely artificial, through wilderness without any settlers and only a few Indians.

Both countries set up commissions, appointed surveyors and astronomers and hired crews of more than 100 workmen. They split the job, with the Americans working from Point Roberts to the Columbia River and the British heading on east from that point.

Of course they checked one another's markers and never came out exactly the same, but they both agreed they were pretty close under the circumstances. The Americans got started in 1857, a year ahead of the British, and finished in 1860.

The British, who had had to pack their supplies from The Dalles up through the Okanogan, staggered out of the woods in 1862. Colonel Hawkins, their leader, was a bit miffed at London, where the auditors could not understand why he had spent so much money on freight charges and on cutting trees.

The two sides had got along fairly well, although they did not agree on what a marker should be. Hawkins held out for iron but Archibald Campbell, who headed the Americans, said iron was too expensive. He made them of stone.

During the original survey a swath was cut only far enough on each side of a marker to allow it to be seen at a distance. The boundary was resurveyed in 1908 and that time it was slashed the whole way, up mountains and down valleys.

Each marker is numbered, starting with an obelisk at the west side of Point Roberts. No. 5 is at the Peace Arch, Ross Lake is bracketed by 71 and 72, and No. 78 is near the Cascade Crest Trail. A monument close to Nighthawk is No. 112.

"New" Marker (1908)
(Right) The 49th Parallel

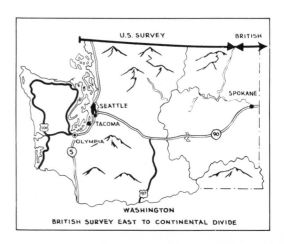

A RARE PLANT
Tweedy Surveyed Flowers, Too

Birdwatchers are delighted when they spot an uncommon specimen, or a common one, for that matter, if it is out of its usual habitat. Wildflowerwatchers are much the same, although they can study their subjects more minutely and never have to hide to do it.

It is unlikely that a birdwatcher in the Pacific Northwest will discover a species that has not yet been named. The odds are against botanists, too, these days, but still there are many mountainous areas whose plants have not been scrutinized scientifically.

Some grow in a very limited area, a fact about them that may not be realized for years. It was back when railroad routes were being surveyed that Frank Tweedy, a member of a surveying team, came across a flower that was not quite like others he had seen.

It belonged to a genus originally collected by the Lewis and Clark expedition and named for Lewis. It was not a species previously identified, though, so it was named for the discoverer—Lewisia tweedyi to be exact, but otherwise known as Tweedy's lewisia.

Other plants first collected by Lewis and Clark, such as camas, ocean spray, Oregon grape and a lewisia best known as bitterroot, were found widely in the Northwest. It was not until recent years that flowerwatchers noticed how exclusive Tweedy's lewisia was. It confined itself almost entirely to the Leavenworth Ranger District of the Wenatchee National Forest.

Being sufficiently rare, it was awarded a reservation of its own. Or if not all its own, at least Tweedy's lewisia was responsible for the designation of a Tumwater Botanical Area in Tumwater Canyon north of Leavenworth. The flowers are up on the hill, growing in crevices and nooks. They run from white to light yellow to peach in color, and bloom in mid-May.

Upstream from the Tumwater Canyon picnic area is the Indian "cave," actually a sheltering boulder that served as a campsite as can be seen from its smoke-blackened roof.

The top side of the canyon can be reached by a steep forest Service Road, No. 2450, which starts in Leavenworth. Another place the flowers can be found is up Swakane Creek, which runs into the Columbia north of Wenatchee but is also in the national forest.

An easy way for a non-botanist to start identifying Lewisia tweedyi or any of the mountain flowers is with a book put out by The Mountaineers, "Wildflowers of Mount Rainier and the Cascades." The pictures are photographs in natural color, large enough for the study of details.

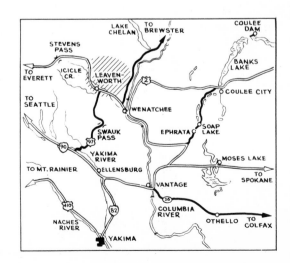

(Lower left) "Indian Cave."
(Below) Here is how the flower looks.

RHODODENDRONS
They Follow the Ancestral Pattern

In contrast to Tweedy's Lewisia (previous subject) rhododendrons comprise one of the largest and most widespread genera on earth. There are hundreds of species, plus all the names and varieties that have come from artificially hybridizing them for gardens.

They may have originated in Asia, but so many millions of years ago that they can be called native to North America by now. Some species have not changed much in all that time, as fossils prove.

In spite of being hardy, long-lived and scattered around the globe, rhododendrons are not naturally adaptable to other than ancestral conditions. That means they like acid soil, preferably peaty. They prefer it to be moist, not wet, and a little shade will do nicely, thank you.

As it happens, those are just the conditions they found along coastal British Columbia and Washington and the Cascades of Oregon. The were so pleased they developed themselves into another species, Rhododendron macrophyllum, with large evergreen leaves and pink blossoms. Some bushes grow to the size of small trees, 20 feet high with a trunk four inches in diameter.

(Right) Macrophyllum, the Pacific Northwest's own rhododendron.

(Lower left) Early blooms, Hood Canal, Olympic Mountains in the background.

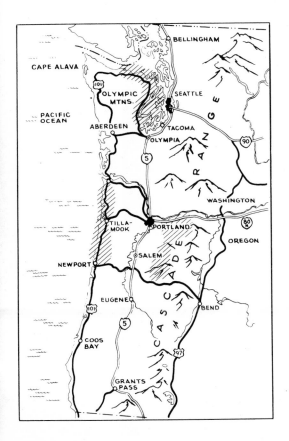

They mass profusely on the Kitsap Peninsula along the east side of Hood Canal, and respond to the western exposure by being the first to bloom in this region, usually by mid-May. That is also when they appear along the Oregon coast.

A week later they are coming out on the west side of the Olympic Peninsula, on Hood Canal and north around the curve to Discovery Bay and Sequim Bay.

At the end of May and the first part of June the unfolding of color reaches the higher elevations of the road to Mt. Hood. Why rhododendrons avoid the Cascades until they cross into Oregon is their own secret. Conditions do not change that much, that humans can see.

The cooler eastern sides of the Olympics are the last to bloom, from the middle to the end of June. The display then is along the higher Forest Service roads, especially along the Quilcene River and Mt. Walker.

The varigated genus is found in many states, particularly in the East and as far south as Georgia, but Washington's naming of the rhododendron as its state flower has good reason. Macrophyllum is far from reprerenting the whole state, but the species does grow most abundantly in Washington.

There is a little-known white rhododendron, too, albiflorum, that appears on wet mountain slopes in British Columbia, Washington, Oregon and over the Northern Rockies. It is more like the azalea type, though, with deciduous leaves.

ELK
They Go Under an Alias

An elk is an elk, a 900-pound animal that nobody who recognizes it from a cow would call a moose or a deer—except the scholars who write encyclopedias. They say an elk is a moose, except in America, where it is a big red deer properly called a "wapiti."

Somebody should tell the game departments. They issue separate hunting tags for elk, moose and deer, as though they were three different animals. And they do not mention a wapiti season.

Of the three creatures, the elk is seen least, although it is numerous in the Pacific Northwest. In Western Canada and Alaska, moose stand in ponds up to their bellies, munching on water plants and staring at passing motorists. Deer pop out of thickets and, especially at night, fatally jump in front of cars to bash up their front ends.

Elk keep out of sight most of the year. They are anti-freeway and stay on the whitest part of maps that show where the human action is.

The most famous elk herd in Washington State lives in the Olympic National Park, where there are only foot trails. They wander out of the park boundaries, but always into country farthest from main highways, like the Lake Ozette area and the Wynootchee River country south of the Olympics.

Another concentration is in the southwest corner of the state, in the Willapa Hills of Pacific and Wahkiakum Counties. They also range in the vicinity of Mt. St. Helens and in the southeast Blue Mountains.

Where they gain the most attention, though, is in the hills and valleys west of Yakima. The winters get cold, snow covers forage and elk temporarily lose their inhibitions.

Hundreds of them come down out of the higher-elevation snow, to the distress of ranchers whose premises they invade to raid haystacks and orchards. The State Game Department therefore feeds them tons of hay until the weather crisis is over.

At the Oak Creek Game Range near Naches, people sometimes outnumber the elk two-to-one in winter, to watch the proceedings. The elk usually hit the breadline in mid-afternoon but do not always set their schedule for sightseers. They may arrive silently during the night and clear out soon after dawn.

Winter breadline on the Elk Range near Naches.

WASHINGTON
HIGHEST CONCENTRATION OF ELK SHADED

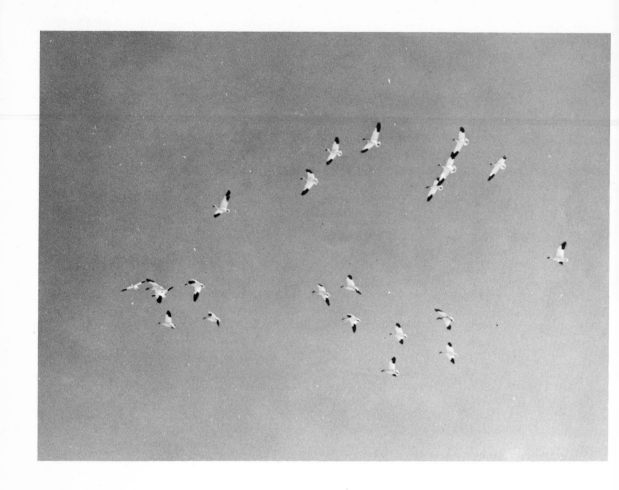

BIRD REFUGES

The areas were set aside as "wildlife refuges," meaning primarily for birds. As urban problems increase, the gag becomes "But what about people refuges?" Maybe that is what the wildlife reservations really are. People can escape to them, too, to live in peace with nature, just looking and not interfering as man usually does.

There are scores of wildlife refuges in the United States set aside by the Fish and Wildlife Service of the Department of the Interior. Almost all are open to visitors. Those who take advantage of them to observe and to shoot pictures, number into the millions every year.

Most of the Washington coast is in refuges with the exception of Grays Harbor. Dungeness and several islands of the San Juans are in the system. On the east side, Toppenish, Conboy Lake, the Columbia River jog at the Saddle Mountains and the vicinity of McNary Dam are among those included. With Turnbull, south of Spokane, there are 14 such refuges in Washington.

Oregon has a dozen including Malheur, described elsewhere. Others are on the coast at Cape Meares, Three Arch Rocks and Oregon Island. On the Willamette Valley side are Baskett Slough, Ankeny and William L. Finley. Down south are Klamath Forest,

Upper Klamath and Lower Klamath. In the northeast are McKay Creek and Cold Springs.

In Idaho there are refuges at Kootenai in the north and Deer Flat down south, with three farther east. Nevada has the same number, aside from a couple of reservations for antelope.

Of all these, the Skagit Game Range between Stanwood and Mount Vernon on the inner Washington coast, is perhaps the most visited by people. It is on the edge of the most populated strip in the Pacific Northwest, and it is open to hunting until the middle of January. If ever birdwatchers and hunters can get along, for a while at least, it is here. Ducks and geese gather by so many thousands that bird-lovers have a hard time arguing that a few fowl cannot be spared to the shooters.

The feature is snow geese. These big birds fly on rather exact schedules to and from the Far North. To them, "going south for the winter" means to Skagit Flats. Apparently they never heard of Hawaii.

Toward the end of April they all leave enmass. Like McBeth's instructions, as quoted by Shakespeare, they "stand not upon the order of your going, but go at once." This makes quite a sight, as well as the sound of thousands of wings flapping at once.

Seeing the birds entails walking along dikes. There are many more species than snow geese. All kinds of ducks, wigeons, scaups, hawks, killdeer, blackbirds and tule wrens make these channels and swampland their home. Sometimes even snowy owls come here for a visit to what they think is the tropics.

Snow geese in formation

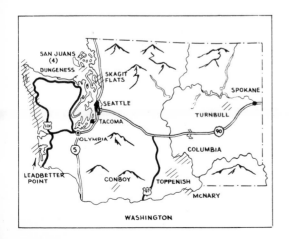

WASHINGTON

OREGON

MIMA MOUNDS
A Mysterious Case of Hives

Before Interstate 5 by-passed them, the "Tenino Mounds" were a familiar sight to travelers on Highway 99. The strange round humps, four to six feet high, covered several miles of natural prairie. Their total acreage has been reduced by farms, highways and other encroachments but they still stand by the tens of thousands. A movement is afoot to preserve them.

Mysterious earth mounds are a natural challenge to human curiosity and the first white explorers dug into them, rather expecting to find Indian burials. Nothing but gravel and some black soil showed up.

Even if bones and artifacts had been exhumed, it still would not have explained the origin of the mounds. It would merely have shown that they were used for human purposes because they were already there. Man-made, they would have to be built at the rate of 1,000 a year for a thousand years, and there were never that many Indians in the country.

Faced with the disappointment that the mounds had no archeological significance, everybody but geologists lost interest in them. The soil was not much good for farming, and until bulldozers came along it was too much work to flatten it out.

Geologists have continued to puzzle over the mounds, now known as "Mima," without ever coming to agreement. They have propounded widely divergent theories, among them these: The glaciers of the last Ice Age terminated just south of Tenino, and in melting deposited silt and rocks that had gathered in surface depressions of the ice; gophers built the mounds; wild cucumber vines held together patches of earth while glacier runoff washed away surrounding soil (and cucumbers, like the Mima area, do have warts).

It is time some neutral referee put these together as the final explanation of the Mima Mounds' origin, so here you have it.

Wild cucumber seeds washed into the silt and gravel on the surface of the glacial sheet. When the sheet cracked up and melted, the cucumbers were left growing on the ground. Gophers then moved into the prefabbed homes.

Now can anyone explain why the Tenino Mounds suddenly became "Mima"?

(Left) The mounds are a lumpy natural prairie.

(Below) Farm shows size of mounds and also that they can be erased.

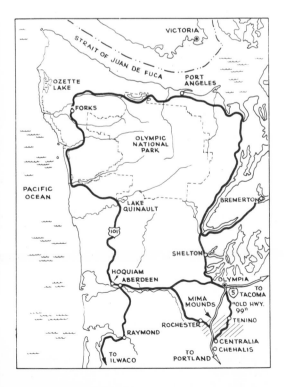

FORT VANCOUVER
Once Capital of the Pacific Northwest

Two keystones of Pacific Northwest history (white settlement division) were Fort Vancouver, now designated as a National Historic Site, and Fort Clatsop, a National Memorial.

Clatsop, near the mouth of the Columbia on the Oregon side, is where Lewis and Clark spent the winter of 1805-06. Between their over land exploration and a goof committed earlier by a British sea captain—who did not recognize a Columbia River when he saw one and thereby left it for an American captain to name—the United States established a solid claim to the territory.

Furthermore, John Jacob Astor beat the British to the river mouth by a few weeks, to set up a fur-trading post at Astoria in 1811. They got it in the war of 1812, but it was returned by treaty. The Hudson's Bay Company thought it over and withdrew to the next most strategic location, Vancouver, opposite the confluence of the Willamette with the Columbia River. The post was started in 1824, with Dr. John McLoughlin as the factor or boss.

He ruled over Oregon Territory, which included Washington and Oregon and which was, by England's definition, all British land.

McLoughlin was no dummy, though. He watched the pushy young Americans pour into Oregon and figured that everything south of the Columbia was a lost cause.

He was their greatest friend when their covered wagon trains arrived sick and broke. In spite of contrary orders from London, he fed them, his men helped them run the river from The Dalles to below the Cascade Falls (see Barlow Pass Road) and all he asked was that they settle south of the river.

He could not stem the tide and in 1846 the international boundary was moved north to the 49th Parrallel, a compromise from the American demand of "54-40 or fight."

Fort Vancouver, which dates from before the Civil War and which saw several famous generals of the Union Army stationed there, is not nearly as interesting, in spite of its preservation, as is the federal visitor's information center on the site of McLoughlin's capital.

It looks down on the flat, long an airfield, where the Hudson's Bay Company had its stockades, stores, farms and manufacturing plants. This was the "city" of the Northwest, rivaling San Francisco, Honolulu and Sitka in the Pacific area as a center of civilization. Vancouver, not Portland, was the Northwest's first Boston.

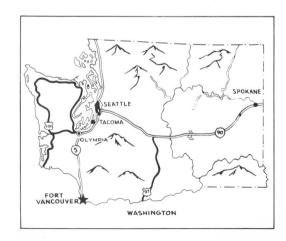

(Left) Marshall House was built in 1886, but its name came from one of the last officers to live in it, Gen. George Marshall.

Dr. John McLoughlin, who started Fort Vancouver, planted appleseeds from London. This ancient tree was born in 1826.

MT. ADAMS LAVA BEDS
A Hot Show Went On Here, Too

In an arc of a few miles from south to west of Mt. Adams, a strange little region exists. It is "little" only in comparison to a similar territory in central Oregon, from McKenzie Pass to Fort Rock, but many of the same geological features are found.

In Oregon the lava flows, ice caves, cinder cones and lava tubes are on or near main highways and are noted and explained by such public agencies as the Forest Service or Oregon State Parks. In Washington, comparable features are far off well-traveled routes, most of them reached only over county, Forest Service or logging roads.

Both Mt. Adams and Mt. St. Helens are recent volcanoes, still classified as dormant. Between them, they roughed up the country for miles around their bases, whether by direct eruptions or with lava that spewed out from fissures miles away.

Above Willard (see "Lassie Lumber Company," following) logging roads climb on through the hills. They skirt around huge patches of terrain whose mean disposition is not apparent at a casual glance because trees do grow on it. But just get out and walk through the scattered timber if you are wearing stout boots and will keep a wary eye on your step.

This area shows on state maps as a patch of dots labeled "Big Lava Beds." It is properly named. Most of the surface is tortuous black rock, sharp, heaved, fallen in sudden holes and cracks. Within a few hundred yards from the nearest road it all looks the same and an explorer easily could get lost.

This is a country of lava tubes. Ape Cave, on the St. Helens side, is more than twice as long as the one Oregon put into a state park south of Bend. Warm humid air enters the collapsed openings of others and meeting their ever-cool interior temperatures, creates snow and year-around ice—natural refrigerators for early-day settlers.

Since the two Northwest states have a plethora of volcanic phenomena, Washington cannot claim this region is unique. There is a certain attraction to it, though, from the lava beds to Trout Lake and vicinity and west to St. Helens, simply because it is off the highway and therefore relatively unknown.

The lava beds, for example, are worthless to loggers and are detoured by them. Who knows what remains to be discovered in their wastes by adventurers who are simply curious?

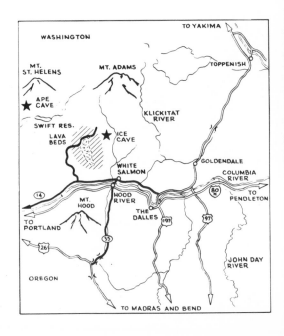

Ice caves are at their best in May. Some visitors later on cannot resist breaking icicles.

(Left) Terrain like this is not an invitation to a long walk in the woods.

LONGEST LOGGING FLUME
It's Owned by the "Lassie Lumber Co."

Back in the 1920's before there were bull-dozers to scrape zigzag roads up mountain-sides so trucks could haul out logs, and the grades were too steep for rails, another idea was tried. Flumes were built to float the logs down.

The nine-mile flume ending in Under-wood, Washington, on the Columbia River, was to serve all the logging companies, but the Easterners who put up the $10,000-a-mile construction cost wanted to charge $3.20 a thousand board feet, high even today. Consequently it was not used enough to turn a profit. The late Harold Broughton, a stock-holder whose lumber mill was at the bottom of the line, took it over.

The flume and the mills at each end are still in the same family. Don Thomas, president of the company and successor to its traditions, declares that the operation will continue indefinitely. Flumes built elsewhere for logs have been abandoned, leaving this one unique.

It can be seen from the Columbia River Highway between Underwood and the side-road to Willard. It is costly to maintain because slides, falling trees and natural deterior-ation knock out sections of it. However, it repays its costs in publicity. An episode in the television show featuring Lassie, that smartest of dogs, was hung on a plot in which the collie and a ranger had to escape from the mountains by riding down the flume on logs.

It could not be done in real life, but with the help of camera angles it was accomplished. The program with its many re-runs gave the Broughton Lumber Co. national publicity and ever since it has been known as "the Lassie Lumber Co." Its salesmen have no problem in identifying themselves to Midwest wholesalers, who want to know about the flume and whether it is still flowing.

It is, and its waters bring down 125,000 board feet of rough-sawed lumber a day to be finished in the lower mill. A plank makes the trip in 55 minutes, so the top mill starts and stops an hour earlier. The flume carries an electric alarm system that signals a break and locates it for repair crews.

It sent the men out in the middle of the night on one false alarm. They finally discovered the trouble. A porcupine had chewed the insulation off a wire.

Rough-cut lumber goes into the flume from the mill at Willard.

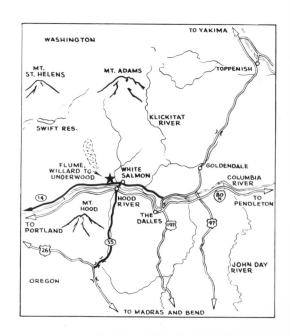

The plank will reach the Underwood mill in 55 minutes, after having traversed nine miles.

BARLOW TOLL ROAD
It Was Better Than Drowning

An irony of the Oregon Trail was that if the emigrants survived starvation, measles, Indians, cholera and general fatigue and arrived at The Dalles, Oregon, they still had the worst mountain range of all to pass through before they got to the Willamette Valley.

The usual route through the Cascades was by way of the Columbia River. It was full of rapids and falls, though, and some who took to boats and rafts drowned before reaching the promised land. At best, wagons had to be taken apart and reassembled on the lower river, and the passage cost money.

Samuel K. Barlow, who led a wagon party to The Dalles in 1845, decided to cross the mountains inland, over the south shoulder of Mt. Hood. His group chopped their way to the summit but there they had to give up in the December snow and continue as a packtrain, without the wagons.

In the spring of 1846 Barlow, backed by a partner, Philip Foster, returned to finish the westside road after first securing the territorial legislature's permission to charge tolls on it. They had it open for that year's arrivals from the east.

Travelers went south from The Dalles to Tygh Valley. There they turned west and in six miles came to the toll gate at Wamic. Staying north of the White River, they climbed to Barlow Pass, 4,155 feet, and came out on the wide saddle between Mt. Hood and Mt. Wilson. On the west, U.S. Highway 26 dashes along much the same course, giving access to Mt. Hood and north-central Oregon. (It does not go through Barlow Pass itself).

As it approaches the summit, the highway passes a replica of a later tollgate, with an old photograph set on a marker stone to show how the site once looked. The road was used by immigrants for nearly 20 years, but as that traffic diminished it was replaced by an unexpected eastbound flow to The Dalles, where those bound for the Idaho goldrushes of the 1860's could catch a boat upriver to Lewiston.

Barlow aimed at the sunset spot south of Mt. Hood.

The wagon party camped at White River crossing.

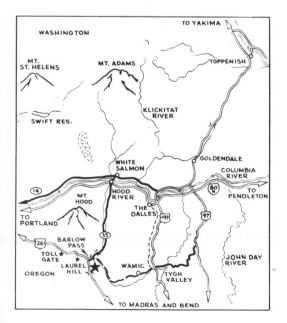

Accounts of the toll charges vary, from $2.50 to $5 a wagon, and from 10 cents a head for livestock to $1. Chances are that wagon tolls did change up and down over so many years, but the $1 a head sounds doubtful. Most early settlers could not afford that much money, especially by the time they reached Oregon.

By going on the eastside Forest Service road or by stopping to explore Laurel Hill just west of the summit, one still can find traces of the original Barlow road, including scars on tree trunks where wagons were roped down the slopes. They had to be hauled up or winched down hillsides at several places.

NACHES PASS
Drowning Might Have Been Better

Washington's first "highway" across the Cascades was toll-free but it never enjoyed the same popularity as Oregon's first crossing, the Barlow Road. To this day it is a rutty trail through the woods, with the ruts more likely to have been made by four-wheel-drive vehicles and trail bikes than by the wagons that used it briefly well more than a century ago.

The Barlow Road was built because the traffic was on its way and pioneers hoped to escape drowning in the Columbia. In 1846, the migration over the Oregon Trail had started. The Naches Pass road, seven years later, was constructed on hopes, stubbornness and, in some respects, for a single wagon train.

Naches Pass rather than Snoqualmie was the most-used Indian trail between eastern and western Washington. The powerful Yakimas lived to the southeast, and the most direct trade route to the Puget Sound country was up the Naches River to its headwaters, then down the Greenwater to the White River. Today's highways detour twice as far, along two legs of a triangle, up the American River to Chinook Pass, then down the White.

The Indian route looked logical to the first white settlers. Even before the Hudson's Bay Company abandoned Fort Nisqually, six miles had been hacked out in that direction.

In 1853 the first governor of Washington Territory, Isaac Stevens, gave the job of laying out a Naches Pass road to a Captain McClellan. McClellan asked expert Indian advice and they, not wanting a traffic jam on their old route, said it was impossible. The captain gave up, but pioneer settlers, hoping to divert some Oregon Trail wagon trains their way, raised $1,200 and hired themselves in two work groups to start building from both the east and the west.

They worked all summer and almost made it. They ran out of money and time—winter was coming—and went home. Then they heard a big wagon train was on its way, counting on the news that a road was there. They rushed back to complete the job.

It was a Herculean task. They had ended the road at a cliff. They met the wagons, 29 to 36 of them depending upon which historical account you read, and helped rope them down the mountainside.

McClellan went up to inspect the job and said the pioneer road builders had done very well. They thought, "We showed you!" But in the long run, Snoqualmie still won out as the logical low pass.

(The Mountaineers' "102 Hikes" covers the whole Naches Trail).

(Left) The shortcut is wide enough to be a challenge to four-wheel drive vehicles.

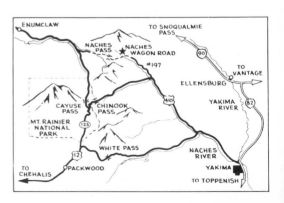

Tree rings show the blaze is about 80 years old. It probably was made by cattlemen using the trail.

COLUMBIA GORGE WATERFALLS
Streams That Don't Meander

Multnomah Falls is so long known and easily seen at a roadside stop on Oregon's Columbia Gorge freeway, it steals the show from what is actually a fine supporting cast. Along a dozen miles of Interstate 80 between Bridal Veil and Eagle Creek just upriver from Bonneville, short trails lead to other waterfalls, any one of which could be a feature attraction.

The Columbia is so wide that "gorge" seems almost a misnomer to motorists speeding along the river level. It isn't, though. Geologically, this section is a phenomenon that may not be duplicated in the world. Rivers everywhere, even the largest, start at range summits and follow paths of least resistance to the sea, detouring for hundreds of miles to get around higher ground.

Granted that the Columbia had a headstart on the Cascade Range, it nevertheless managed an unusual feat. As the mountains rose, the mighty river doggedly chewed its channel at equal pace. Otherwise it would have been deflected into California and Southwest Congressmen would not have to think up plots to pipe it there.

The Gorge is therefore actually a mountain "pass" less than 400 feet above sea level. Its cliffs are a cross-section view of the Cascade's foundation—or at least the top two or three thousand feet. Creeks that elsewhere would twist and meander in long courses down either the east or west slope of the range come to a sudden end when they topple into the big alleyway.

Several of the streams are no more than three miles long, but during their brief run they plunge 2,500 feet. In doing it they make quite a splash. Multnomah Falls is the final 620-foot leap of a four-mile stream that starts at an elevation of more than 3,200 feet.

The area is in the Columbia Gorge District of Mt. Hood National Forest. Casual hikers, taking only an hour or two, can follow the ravines and narrow gorges upward past series of falls. Horsetail Falls is only 1.3 miles off the road. In another mile a hiker can loop back past Oneonta Falls to the highway.

The Eagle Creek trail (this page) taps half a dozen falls in its first six miles. It goes on to join other trails used by overnight backpackers. Camping spots are scattered throughout this area.

Maps are available at the Multnomah Falls Visitor Information Center or from the Columbia Gorge District Ranger Headquarters in Troutdale, Oregon.

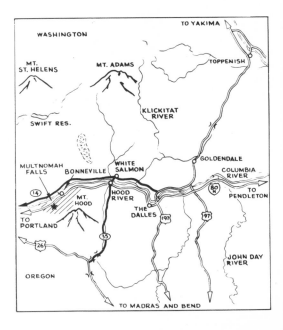

Horsetail Falls is only 1.3 miles from the highway.

(Left) The Eagle Creek trail leads to several falls.

HORSETHIEF LAKE
The Region's First Shopping Center

Horsethief Lake, on the Columbia River a couple of miles above The Dalles Dam, is a recent addition to Washington's park system, but probably no state park in the nation has been used longer as a camping and outdoor recreation site. Can any place else beat 10,000 years?

Technically speaking, archeologists exploring the Horsethief Lake area never got back that far before the dam flooded their diggings. Right across the river, though, their findings delivered a carbon-14 test date of 9,785 years. Since the smaller Oregon settlement had been a suburb of Wakemap, it is reasonable to suppose the Washington village was even older.

There were many ancient villages along the Columbia, but the most heavily populated area east of the Willamette River was at the entrance of the "Long Narrows," five miles above today's city of The Dalles. There the Columbia squeezed into a broiling channel less than 100 yards wide and salmon running upriver could be caught by the ton.

An early reporter of the scene estimated that the permanent census might be as few as 100 Indians, but that up to 3,000 gathered when the salmon were at the peak of their run. Most Indians, he said, were not there to fish but to trade, gamble and gossip. They came from the coast and from far inland. No matter what their tribal enmities, a king's-X prevailed at this point.

The stretch of rapids was a political and economic Switzerland. Several neighboring tribes were powerful enough to wipe out the resident Wishrams and take over, but then what? Interminable wars would have ensued. So the Indians gathered there in peace, century after century.

The Dalles Dam submerged Celilo Falls, the historic fishing spot a dozen miles above the dam, in 1957. It is now commemorated only by a small county park on the Oregon side. The Indian village of Wishram was below the falls. Lewis and Clark described it and so did Washington Irving, in "Astoria."

The Wishrams (another spelling is "Wishham") owned the fishing sites and passed

Horsethief Butte is a landmark as you head downriver from Maryhill on the Washington side.

(Right) "She-Who-Watches" looked down on a now-submerged village.

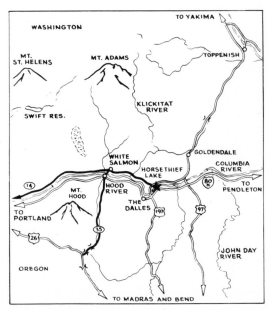

them along, generation to generation. Visitors, whether from across the river or from a distance, were allowed to use the sites as long as they made no claim to ownership.

The Wishrams were the Mid-columbia Merchants Association. Their small territory was the Northwest's first shopping center. The permanent residents were scattered in sub-villages of four to 20 houses. One such settlement, between the present dam and Horsethief Lake, was called Spearfish—which may or may not have been the Indian word for it. The village was around the downstream corner of the state park. So too was Wakemap Mound ("Wok-em-up"), probably the most ancient archeological site in the state until the Marmes discovery in the Palouse—also flooded by a dam.

Lewis and Clark noted the height of the mound. It was later measured as 350 feet long, 270 feet wide and at least 20 feet deep. It was a midden, built up from century upon century of encampment on the same spot. Indians tended to built partially subterranean shelters. And they, too, were litterbugs. The wind blows up the Columbia River Gorge much of the time, so no doubt when they returned each year, they had a fresh sand floor. Eventually they had to raise the roof.

The Indians used a flat just above The Narrows (named Colowesh Bottom by the whites, for a chief who must have sat there a long time) as a campground.

During the fishing and social season, they arrived by the hundreds and this was the broadest open space along the narrow river banks. As it happened, it was also where a natural trail from the north reached the river.

The annual salmon run, the corresponding movement of the Indians over milleniums and the intertribal rules that developed led to the attachment of religious connotations to the area. It may have been a place of sharp mercantile practices (as Lewis and Clark noted in explaining their expense account for provisions and horses purchased there) but it also was "sacred."

Undoubtedly that was why it became a burial ground, not only for those who had lived their lives on the river's edge or who died by circumstance while they were there, but who were brought from afar to be buried.

Graves rim the basaltic walls facing the river. Most burials, though, were on islands, several of which were named Memaloose, the Chinook word for dead. Upper Memaloose, one of the two most important, can be seen to the east from Horsethief Butte, part of the state park.

It is just a sandbar now. Before the dam submerged the island, the bones of 2,500 Indians with everything that had accompanied them to the grave were removed and placed in a vault in a cemetery near the Washington end of The Dalles bridge.

The concrete-slab covered vault is not an inspiring monument to such a long history of mankind. Neither is the surrounding heavy wire fence, a result of bitter experience. Since an Indian's belongings were buried with him, for many years graves have been dup up by souvenir hunters.

Horsethief Lake is doubly man-made. It was formed when The Dalles Dam backed water into Colowesh Bottom. In addition, its south "shore" is the railroad fill that separates the lake from the Columbia except by culverts.

Its name is of uncertain origin. There is a story about a nearby hidden coulee where horsethieves corraled their loot. It also may be assumed that when so many horseback tribes camped near each other here, some pilfering from the parking lots was inevitable. In Indian tradition, horse stealing from strangers was a way to win honors.

However, Horsethief Lake, Horsethief Butte or Horse Point, the name obviously is recent. There were no horses around the area during the first 9,700 years of its history. The animals arrived after the Spaniards penetrated the Southwest.

Besides fishing, trading and gambling the profits, when the Indians gathered here, they also went in for art. The sheer rock faces both up- and downriver from the lake were just right for painted pictographs and chipped-in-the-stone petroglyphs. Most of these were submerged by the dam but a few of the higher ones, above the railroad tracks, still exist.

One painting, "She-Who-Watches," is so unusual it rates as sort of a pictograph Mona Lisa. Explanations of such pictures should be listened to with reservations at this late date. Pressed by eager whites to produce a story to go with drawings that are a mystery to them, too, Indians oblige.

Accordingly, "She Who Watches" was once No. 1 Woman in the Spearfish village below. Coyote, top god of Indian legend, changed her into the rock above town where she could keep an eye on things. But don't quote it as the last word on the subject.

The north side of Horsethief Butte is so steep mountaineer groups use it to train novices, and the rocks bear unretrieved pitons. You can easily hike up, though, especially from the southwest corner where the sand has been riddled by pothunters illegally looking for Indian campsites and graves.

Aside from the sweeping view of the gorge and Mt. Hood from several "summits," the butte is split up in a fascinating maze of little coulees. Any one of them could be the hideout of—well, horsethieves.

Mt. Hood through a defile on Horsethief Butte.

The commandant's home is fully restored and furnished as in this kitchen. The house is flanked by remaining officers' quarters. Other buildings, now gone, are outlined on the grounds.

(Right) The cannon never shot at anybody, but it probably impressed the Indians.

FORT SIMCOE
The Indians Let You Visit It

The Indian wars of Eastern Washington had been fought and won or lost—by Indians or by U.S. troops—before Fort Simcoe was built out in the lovely valley west of Yakima. The creek and the grove were an oasis for Indians, and the low pass to the south connected the inland country to the Columbia River near The Dalles.

Col. Granville O. Haller attempted to march north from The Dalles in 1855 and the Indians whupped him in the Simcoe Mountains. He barely got back to the river, leaving behind a cannon. Not only did the colonel have to report a defeat, but also the loss of his artillery. Apparently it was retrieved later, but to this day cannon hunters ignore the record and go looking for it.

After the shooting was over, the Army began building Fort Simcoe. If you think "overrides" on the contract costs of military construction are something new, you should have been around more than a century ago. The brick, the glass, the carved mantels and moldings for the fort were hauled by wagon from The Dalles where some of the materials had arrived from the East Coast, around the Horn of South America.

In general, wooden buildings in the Pacific Northwest not maintained year to year quickly deteriorate because of the weather but Fort Simcoe, in a dry part of the state, is an exception. The commandant's house and flanking quarters for officers still stand at the south end of the old quadrangle.

There were blockhouses at four corners of the compound that took in barracks, parade grounds, supporting facilities such as a blacksmith shop and, naturally, a jail. Only one of the original blockhouses still stands. The rest are replicas. The logs of the one original, which was modified for a stable, have been whittled by souvenir hunters looking for bullets—a futile endeavor, because nobody ever fired at the fort.

Almost as soon as the fort was finished, it was (in modern terms) declared "surplus." It was turned over to the Rev. James Wilbur, Indian Agent, who ran things for 20 years thereafter.

Fort Simcoe's preservation and its status as a Washington State park are due to the tolerance of the Yakima Indians. It is well inside the Yakima Indian Reservation. The fort was built to help subdue them, but a visitor gets to it only through strictly controlled land of the Yakima Nation.

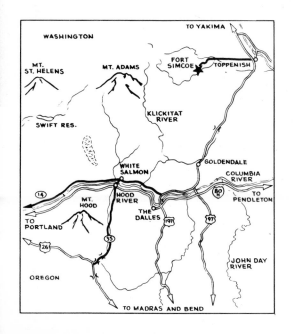

GINKGO PETRIFIED FOREST
Sustained Yield Program Takes Time

The Pacific Northwest, logging its Douglas fir, pine, hemlock and spruce, it not noted for hardwoods. However, one of the world's hardest forests is found in a central Washington state park. A veritable arboretum, it includes some 50 genera and 200 species, all in stone.

It is possible through planting and natural seeding to reforest logged-off land and produce another softwood crop in from 50 to 100 years. Sustained yield also can be achieved with petrified forests but it takes longer, a few million years.

The established method for producing petrified logs is to start with a flat plain, well watered, and grow trees upon it. When a mature stand has developed, cover it with lava. Lava came naturally in the Pacific Northwest, 15 to 20 million years ago, simply pouring up from fissures in the ground.

From the conservation standpoint, lava could be criticized as wasteful of natural resources. Being so hot, it burned most of the timber. However, there always were fallen trees buried in the mud or waterlogged in a lake. They sizzled, but their moisture also cooled the lava and they remained whole.

If there had been only one lava flow, geologists would have found only a Ginkgo Petrified Grove. However, the process was repeated time and again with such long intervals between, lava turned to soil and grew another forest. Streams carried driftwood of many species into lakes, thus gathering a fine collection for the next hot burial.

That was the logging method. Processing also required many centuries as water seeped down through the lava beds and replaced wood fiber with silica. Finally, when the logs were ready, they had to be re-exposed by thousands of years of erosion. They were worth waiting for, though. No other trees grace the arid hills near Vantage.

"Ginkgo" was the name given to the whole area, of which some 6,000 acres is in the state park, because the primitive specie was found among the stony logs. In human history ginkgos never have existed in the wild and were preserved only in China as a rare ornamental tree.

The state park's interpretive center at Vantage is always worth a stop. Aside from the geologic story, it presents a sweeping view of the Columbia River in its basaltic gorge.

(Left) The pictographs were going to be drowned under the backwater of Wanapum Dam so they were chunked off a Columbia River wall and placed at the Ginkgo interpretive center.

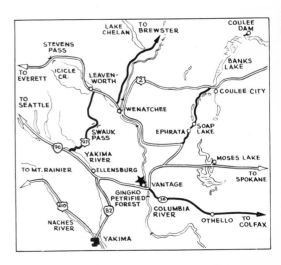

Much of the 6,000-acre state park is closed to ran-
dom visitation to save petrified trees like this from
souvenir hunters. However, students on legitimate
scientific business can get entrance permits.

MOSES COULEE

Moses Coulee, second largest to Grand Coulee, ends with a sudden right-turn outlet into the Columbia gorge between Wenatchee and Quincy, thereby screening itself from passersby on State Highway 28, who glimpse its mouth as a basin laced with power poles. Since no main road runs the length of the canyon, most motorists get a view of it only where U.S. Highway 2 crosses it half way between Waterville and Coulee City.

Being off the traffic path puts the few residents of Moses Coulee in an enviable position. They are hidden away, uncrowded, in a walled valley of Western scenery that includes a creek, but the outlet road is straight, level and hard surfaced for more than a dozen miles so "outside" towns are quickly reached. Their own village, Palisades, is midway in the 18-mile stretch of the lower coulee. Its liveliest businesses are the post office and the school.

Moses Coulee appears to end at a wall broken on either side by ravines. Here the road must leave the valley, swinging sharply up the hill to the east. It comes out on the plateau and joins a blacktopped road.

Along here Moses Coulee went to potholes. Northbound, the road detours it for five or six miles. The badlands being worthless for anything else, they are now subdivided as "Rimrock Meadows." The only building in sight is a new real estate office, open week-ends.

When the upper coulee becomes defined, the road once again drops into the channel, skirting irrigated ranches. To insure rain, one rancher simply hung the pipes crosswise overhead, anchoring them at the top of the rock walls.

At U.S. Highway 2, the continuation of the road is at the eastern edge of the coulee. It leads to Jamison Lake—or Jameson or Jamieson, depending upon which map or road sign you consult.

Thirty years ago the lake's name was not spelled at all. It was a horse-grazing meadow. After Banks Lake, the Grand Coulee holding reservoir 20 miles east, had filled, water rose in upper Moses Coulee. An attempt to build a road around the precipitous sides resulted in a slide, making this the end of the line.

The State Game Department stocks the lake with trout. Fishermen are not allowed to camp along the shore and there are no facilities except toilets.

(Below) Road and (right) ranch in lower Moses Coulee.

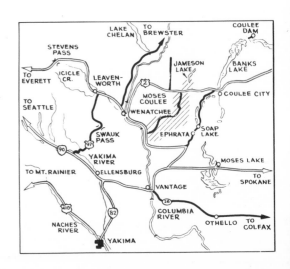

Columnar basalt is common in coulee walls.

THIS MOSES NEVER LED HIS
PEOPLE TO THEIR PROMISED LAND

The man who left his name on the coulee, a nearby lake and a city was, in his own way, as famous a chief as Seattle, Joseph or Sitting Bull. He controlled hundreds of warriors in the Columbia Basin but he was not a fighting hero. He was not too friendly to the whites but neither was he an overt enemy. He just kept them guessing.

Moses was a hereditary chief who inherited his empire from his father. He kept it longer than most Indians managed to, through a combination of brains, physique, diplomatic skill and a sense of humor. He was born about 1829 and died in 1899.

His domain was the middle stretch of the Columbia, from Waterville down to White Bluff, and he was such a superb horseman he could turn up at either end the same day. Undoubtedly one of his "freeways" was Moses Coulee, a channeled shortcut from near Waterville to the river below Wenatchee.

After other Indians had been put on the Yakima reservation or the Colville, Moses continued to roam independently east of the Columbia. Being so powerful and footloose, he caused the white settlers no end of anxiety at each scare of Indians going on the warpath, and he was blamed in gossip for whatever went wrong.

More thoughtful comments by pioneers who knew him are tinged with a tone of admiration. How Moses operated was described in an old publication by A. J. Splawn, a cattleman who had won the chief's respect and vice versa.

Chief Joseph had jumped the reservation to make his long-remembered trek northeast, defeating pursuing troops at each encounter. He urged Moses to join him in an uprising, and the next thing white settlers saw was that Indians had gathered in encampments along the Columbia for miles. From a count of lodges it was estimated that 2,000 warriors had assembled and there may have been another 1,000 to 1,500 back in the coulees.

The greatly outnumbered settlers holed up in forts and might nervously have shot any innocent Indian who came within range, thus setting off a war in which they probably would have been wiped out. Splawn and another man went to ask Moses for a parlay.

Moses, honoring their solitary bravery, crossed the Columbia to meet them. He said he was not going to attack. He spoke candidly, that his people might win temporary victories but would lose in the long run. He even revealed his strategy for avoiding a war.

He had summoned all the tribes so they would be encamped within his daily riding range, where he could keep track of them. He held them for some three weeks until the settlers had relaxed and his own hotheads had cooled off, then sent them home.

There were other crises that Moses met with aplomb. When a scraggly posse invaded his territory to arrest several of his tribesmen, the chief confronted them with horsemen who approached in the well-drilled maneuvers of the U.S. Army and silently faced off the posse with rifles at the ready. The posse backed down, leaving Moses to handle the situation.

He was promised a reservation of his own but when he came to Yakima for a conference, he was promptly taken into custody and narrowly missed assassination. He went to Washington, D.C., in 1879 and again in 1883 and each time was "awarded" a land for his people. Each time the government reneged and he ended up on the Colville Reservation, along with Chief Joseph.

The two probably carried on many an argument about whether they should have joined forces. By the time Moses died, no longer a threat, he was accepted fondly by some of his old friends. Joseph the fighter is more famous, but Moses' name lasts too, as a man whose decisions avoided much bloodshed that would not, in the end, have changed history.

Jameson Lake was once a meadow.

DRY FALLS
It Didn't Stay in One Place

Grand Coulee Dam still stands as one of the hugest constructions ever completed by the human race. The Great Pyramid of Giza would make a cornerstone in it, but adding eight more Great Pyramids would leave the dam either lower or leaking.

Aside from the power Grand Coulee Dam produces, it altered nature by creating a lake 150 miles long in back of it, and for more than 100 airline miles to the south it changed a million-and-a-quarter acres from desert to farmland.

A good place to stand while thinking in awe about what wonders man hath wrought is in the observatory at Dry Falls, designated as a federal natural landmark as well as a state park. Older Grand Coulee Dams diverted the water down this channel and over the falls. The last one was more than three times the height of today's dam and 50 times larger in bulk. It was an arm of the ice sheet that covered Canada and moved as far south as the river.

At least three Ice Ages contributed to the erosion of the Columbia Basin by blocking the river and pouring torrents south when the glaciers melted. However, the first time Dry Falls ran out of water, it was down by Soap Lake.

The general pattern of the drainage maze had been established before the last Ice Age. As seasonal and cyclical floods diminished, higher channels ran dry and the runoff continued in the biggest and oldest coulees. When the last ice dam pushed its way out of the Okanogan, Grand Coulee was off and roaring again.

The abrasive used in cutting out coulees was a mixture of silt, boulders and chunks of ice. When dumped 400 feet in a waterfall, it was rough on the retaining wall, too. The wall kept crumbling and in a short time, perhaps no more than 6,000 years, the falls at Soap Lake had moved up to its present site, leaving a 20-mile canyon behind it.

The same thing had occurred up the river. A falls as large and even higher cut itself back almost to the overflow point at the Columbia, where it ran into harder rock and tapered off as the grand-daddy of all rapids. It left upper Grand Coulee in its wake. That is why we do not have two Dry Falls, but Coulee City lost nothing in the exchange. Between Ice Ages it had a Dry Falls above it, now it has one below.

(Right) Aerial view of Dry Falls, with Banks Reservoir, upper coulee, above. (Left) Near Deep Lake there is an old stagecoach road that led to Coulee City.

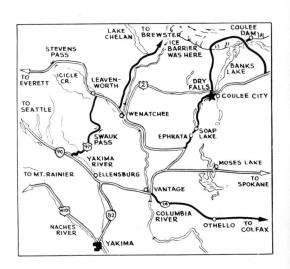

The Columbia is a mighty river but only a pigmy compared to its size in the old days. Both its waterfalls set all-time world records. The one at Dry Falls was three miles wide, with water 50 to 300 feet deep pouring over the edge. It could have run two Niagaras in every state of the Union, all of them two-and-a-half times higher.

Falling debris carved deep holes at the foot of the falls, wherever it happened to be at the moment. These became basins for lakes that enhance the scene and add to the attrac-tion of Sun Lakes State Park below Dry Falls. The new interpretive center overlooking the basin is a dandy, and ridding the site of a souvenir store that sold keepsakes from the Orient was also an improvement. The information to be absorbed at the center goes beyond geology into early human habitation and an explanation of the Lake Lenore trails and caves.

It is hard to think of an easier roadside stop that offers so much so quickly, even to those who have made the stop many times.

BLUE LAKE RHINO
A Bad Day in Black Rocks

A rather small prehistoric rhinoscerus named Diceratherium (or perhaps Aphelops) once lived in what later became central Washington. It was having a bad day among the black rocks. Air pollution was terrible. It was smoky, and sulphurous fumes smelled worse than the Tacoma pulp mill. Green space was rapidly disappearing under blacktop. Its thick flowing advance turned lakes and streams into steam, which then mixed with the smoke and became smog. The whole ecology was going to pot.

So was the weather. It wasn't just the humidity, it was the heat. Diceratherium plodded into a pond in an attempt to keep cool. The lava kept coming closer but there really was no place to escape it. "I might as well become an extinct species," Diceratherium sighed, and sank to the bottom of the water, never more to rise.

"Never more"? A dramatic phrase, but in a few million years it proved to be untrue. Protecting water chilled the lava around Diceratherium (or maybe Aphelops—too few

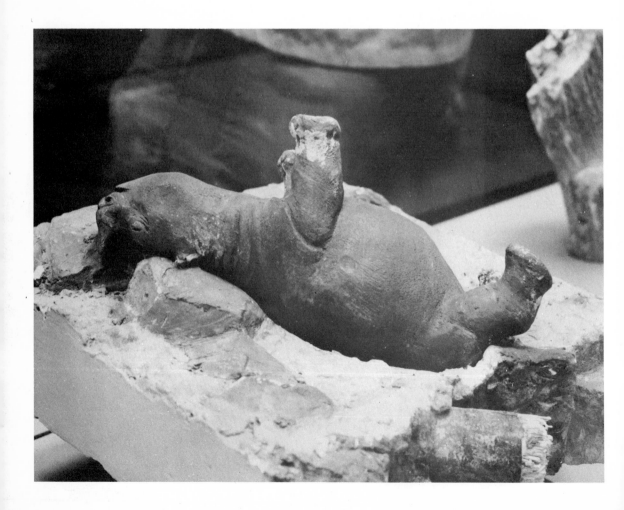

bones were found to make certain of the species) and the ancient rhino's form was preserved in basalt.

More lava, hundreds of feet, were piled on top, but eventually the reverse process set in and erosion cut channels down past the animal's tomb. By the time it was discovered in 1933, it was 200 feet high on a cliff in Jasper Canyon, at the end of Blue Lake.

Rock tumbling from the face of the cliff had exposed a small hole. Two Seattle couples, following a ledge that had once been the lake bottom, peered in and concluded it was a mighty odd-shaped cave. They removed a jaw fragment with teeth, and presented the find to the University of Washington, which in turn gave the bones to Prof. George Beck of Central Washington State College, an expert on the geology of the region.

Many geologists and paleontologists have studied the bone fragments and the unique cave since then, and students tackled the job of making a mold from it. A small cast from the mold is on exhibit at the Dry Falls Visitors Center, along with the interpretive story.

Although the cave is not readily accessible, innumerable visitors have found their way across or around Blue Lake into Jasper Canyon, and up along the wall. The more adventurous try it on for size but (fortunately) always fit into it too loosely. The rhinoscerus was close to eight feet long, with a waist measurement about the same.

Along the cliff-hanging trail are molds of trees that disintegrated after the lava cooled around them, and at least one log that petrified instead. They appear on the same sedimentary line between lava flows on which the rhino lay, lending support to the theory of how the animal escaped cremation. (See Ginkgo Petrified Forest).

(Left) Rhino lies in state, as a cast, at Dry Falls interpretive center.
(Right) Students try the cave for fit.

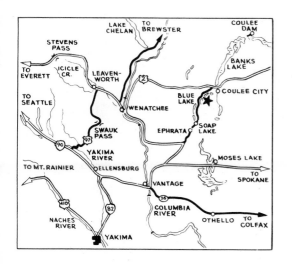

HIDDEN COULEES
Places to Carry Snakebite Kits

A maze of coulees is found in the Upper Columbia Basin, around its rim and on its south edges. Most— but not all—of them have roads like this penetrating them.

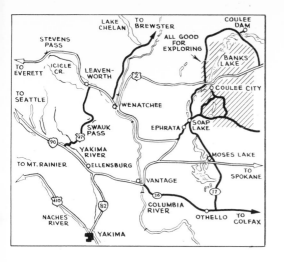

You cannot see the lower end of the coulee from a highway because it is "hanging." That is, it quits in what looks like a low skyline indistinguishable from the rest of the hills. Its upper end is lost in the maze of gorges spreading south across the Columbia Basin, among which Moses and Grand Coulee are only two.

A friend who was born and grew up in the area, and who still lives there, told us about it. Furthermore he took us in his Jeep to set us loose in it, passing on the way through a rancher's barbed wire fence. It was private property, but maybe the rancher was his cousin. We did not ask.

Once we got over what had looked like merely a low ridge, we were in the coulee. However, its sides suddenly came together, sheer and impenetrable, blocking further progress. Our friend drove to the end of the basin and stopped. We got out of the vehicle and he led us to the wall. Unless you knew

where the break was and were right upon it, the passage through was hidden.

We climbed up through that narrow niche and another one, and came out on a broad valley stretching miles into the distance—a hidden, roadless coulee with walls hundreds of feet high.

"There is a way out," our friend said, pointing to two butte formations on the top of the coulee wall several miles away. "Go there and you will find a trail up between them and down the other side to a road. I'll meet you at the bottom there this afternoon."

With a young son we set off exploring, stepping over the bleached bones of a cow that had died on the faint trail. It was a weird land, with little coulees in the big coulee, round potholes unseen until one was a few feet away from the edge, rattlesnakes, desert plants and the incongruous butte rimmed by rocks, plainly man-piled, mentioned under "Rockwall Mysteries."

Indians followed the coulee channels in their migrations and camped in caves in the rock cliffs.

Campers here had a cozy nook with a picture window overlooking Lake Lenore.

A short distance from the butte was a blackly weather-beaten ranch house, starkly naked in the desert and long abandoned.

There were caves in the coulee walls. We poked into one of them, 50 feet above the level of the plain. Rock falling from the cliffs above had all but sealed the entrance so it was necessary to climb over a ridge and down into the shelter.

Someone had been there before us, digging into the floor of the cave to find out whether somebody had used it as a shelter long before the diggers came along. Since so many holes had been made already, we also scratched out some dirt and rock to see what the excavators were looking for.

It took no trained archeologist to learn the answer. In a few fistfuls of earth we turned up the charcoal of campfires, rotted bits of

matting with needle holes in the reed fibers, and broken bones of birds and animals that probably lived in the cave.

We left it at that and the chances are that nobody else meanwhile has disturbed the cave any more than we did. It would not be an important archeological find. Coulee walls throughout the Basin are full of such shelters that were used by Indians as they followed the same path of least resistance taken by the Ice Age runoff waters that cut these valleys.

Down Grand Coulee, below Sun Lakes State Park, seven such shelters have been marked for the curious to visit by short hikes. These caves are of the same erosion origin as the one at the Marmes site (pages 78 and 79) but so far they have not revealed such a long story of human habitation.

POTHOLES LAKE
You Can Have An Island to Yourself

The State of Washington was in a peculiar position. It had some fine beaches but no water to go with them. This was unfortunate because the beaches were on the sunny but arid side of the Cascades, where they would be especially appreciated.

Along came the federal Bureau of Reclamation, irrigating the flat areas of the Columbia Basin. It needed a reservoir, which required a dam to hold the water, so it chose a site for both that was no good as farmland. It lay south of Moses Lake, where the plain broke up into potholes and small coulees. An earth dam three and a half miles long was built through them and the reservoir submerged those on the upper side.

The O'Sullivan dam, completed in 1950, was high enough to back water north into the beach area, which until then had looked like an expanse of sand dunes. The rising lake surrounded hundreds of humps, turning each one into an island, and what delights boaters, water skiers and campers is that every one is an unnamed desert island.

It would be better, of course, if each island had a couple of palm trees, but so far no federal or state agency has moved to make that improvement. Perhaps it is because

shoreline recreation areas hold a priority and the first state park is only now being developed at the southwest corner of the lake.

Other considerations are that while summers are hot enough for palm trees, winters aren't; and that the size, shape and lifetime of an island are not entirely predictable. The wind used to keep the sand piled up, but now it blows the exposed tops into the water.

Ducks and geese looked upon the lake as an airport built for them and changed their migratory flight habits accordingly. Other birds nest along the shorelines and the potholes remaining below the dam.

The lower potholes turned out to be a bonus to fishermen. Luckily, the ground leaks a bit, as the engineers expected it would, and water seeps through subterranean cracks to rise in coulee depressions. Ponds are now scattered through badlands that went dry thousands of years ago.

Fish are plentiful in Potholes Lake, especially perch and crappie. Other species are bluegill, trout, bass, occasional catfish and beer cans. Fishermen keep the lake and its shores stocked with the last one.

Campers on the island should bring their own water supply and, until the palm trees are planted, their own shade.

(Left) Desert islands by the hundreds and (below) campers taking advantage of them.

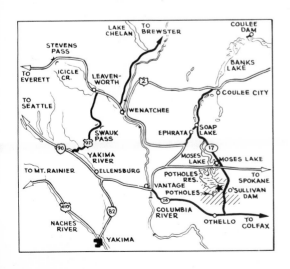

A VERY MEAN INDIAN

At the top of the long grade from the Yakima valley on the highway to Satus Pass and Goldendale, there is a fenced enclosure. Years ago it had a pile of stones in it, somewhat in the shape of a spread-eagled human form. Most of the rocks are gone now, and equally mysterious holes about a foot deep have appeared. According to a local story, the rocks have been replaced many times.

The tale told about this spot is that innumerable moons ago one of the Indians living in the area grew into a giant about 12 feet tall. His size was matched only by his meanness. Nobody could get along with him. Fed up with his trouble-making, the tribe ganged up as David and killed Goliath. They buried him in what is now the fenced area.

He was too mean to stay dead. He dug his way out, and being peeved at the others for what they had done, was worse than ever. So they killed him again and piled stones on his grave to hold him down. He dug out a second time, twice as mean.

His suffering tribesmen held council and came up with a bright idea. The third time they did him in, they planted him face downward, with the rocks on his back.

The way the rocks disappear (sinking?) he must have continued his activities, but if he ever clawed out, it was in China. So there is no use to try to disprove the story by looking for him in the enclosure today.

The fenced area is seen from the old highway. The new one sweeps by just to the west, carefully missing the "grave." It had to be graded to a lower level and the engineers took no chance of unearthing a lot of trouble.

Indians were supposed to help the cause of peace by placing a heavy rock on the giant's outline. The rocks keep disappearing.

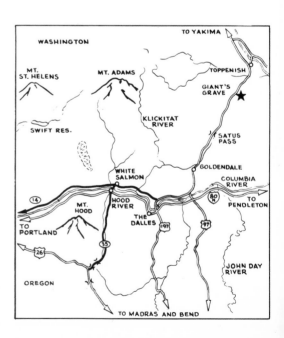

ROCKWALLED MYSTERIES

Anyone exploring coulees and buttes afoot may come across basaltic rock walls, obviously man-made. They are loosely piled and not more than two or three feet high, so they were not meant for corrals. Furthermore, they often meander in apparently aimless fashion.

Who stacked the stones? Sometimes a reasonable deduction is that it was a rancher, when the low barricades are across a break in a coulee wall. Cattle grazing their way up a small draw could be discouraged from going farther. From below, looking upward, two feet added to a steep slope could appear insurmountable.

But what about the stones placed on the rim of buttes? Were they to keep cattle from going near the edge and falling off? Or were they an ammunition dump, gathered in case Indians had to ward off the approach of hostile climbers? We found the top of a small steep-sided butte that rises in the middle of a remote coulee ringed with one-man rocks.

For many years, crumbling rock walls, cairns and pits scooped from a lonely talus slope above the Columbia River Highway east of White Salmon, Washington, have been a mystery to the few persons who come across them.

The ancient walls, three to five feet high and covering some ten acres, show no pattern, enclose nothing, were indefensible as fortifications, contain no buried artifacts and are disclaimed by the local Indians.

In many tribes, when a young Indian approached manhood, he was sent to a remote spot to seek a guardian spirit. Perhaps the stones were stacked as part of the ritual. An unattached spirit could see that here was a worthy candidate. It took both strength and determination to carry heavy stones on the hot arid slope without benefit of food or water. Under such circumstances, it also was quite possible for the spirit-seeker to end up with the necessary visions.

The talus slope was far enough from the Wishram village at Celilo Falls to qualify as "remote," but close enough that a medicine man might quietly wander over and check the work. There's nothing like a stone wall for permanent proof.

Since the guardian spirit was a very personal matter, it was no business of curious white men who came along later and asked questions. The Indians professed ignorance.

At least that's one theory about the stone walls.

Who stacked the stones?

BATTLE BUTTE
A Peaceful Place

Long-settled Klickitat County has its duly billed points of interest, from the skiing area at Satus Pass to Maryhill Castle and incongruous Stonehenge, but among its best attractions are its serenity and a quick-change act, neither of which is the sort of thing you find explained on roadside signs or historic markers.

Stretched 75 airline miles west to east, from forested Cascades to arid hills, the county contains too much variety to characterize it from any one viewpoint. The band through the center, though, where U.S. 97 runs, borrows from both sides and the combination gives it park-like quality north of Goldendale.

The forest around 3,149-foot Satus Pass gives away to meadows and groves, followed by open basins and wheat ranches and finally the sparse grazing land on the hills and cliffs above the Columbia. All that change is in 25 miles.

Rocky buttes seem to extend an invitation to climb them so the whole panorama can be taken in at once. Battle Butte, standing alone on the dividing line between trees and open ranchland, is the best of these. Its name is connected to no known incident in Indian or white history, but arrowheads long were found along a creek near its base (because Indians used to camp there) and the butte's walls, terraces and flat circular top suggest a fort.

It is on private land, a ranch being worked by the third generation while the fourth generation plays in the yard. The young owners, Marvin and Donna Norris, look mildly upon climbers of their butte as long as the visitors mind their manners and don't leave gates open.

From the top the horizon is dominated on the southwest by Mt. Hood, while due west Mt. Adams is massively exposed from base to summit. From a butte across the valley and at one point on the highway south of Goldendale, Mt. St. Helens and Mt. Rainier are added to the view.

In the large photograph, right, the closest trees below are on a high bench. While climbing down from it in mid-day we startled a herd out of one grove into another. There were nine of them, all deer.

Below, Mt. Adams and, right, Mt. Hood from Battle Butte.

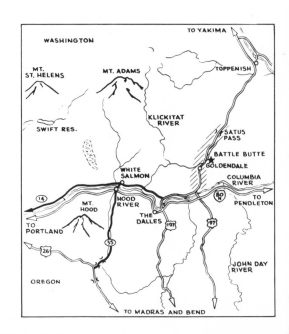

MARYHILL AND STONEHENGE
What Was in Sam Hill's Idea Anyway?

Maryhill Castle, and Stonehenge five miles east of it, are monuments to eccentricity backed by a lot of money. Imported Belgian Quakers, the replica of so-called Druid ruins from England, a castle of German architecture turned into a museum featuring the Queen of Romania, all on arid cliffs overlooking the Columbia, are not a combination explained by easy logic.

Multimillionaire lawyer Samuel Hill put up cabins for the Quakers but they could not make a living from the rocky soil and moved away. The castle, started in 1913, apparently was inspired by a type seen along the Rhine. Mary was Hill's wife but neither of them ever lived in the place. Queen Marie of Romania "dedicated" the unfinished building in 1926, but not as a museum. That designation came in Hill's will, when he died in 1931. The museum opened in 1940.

As for Stonehenge, Hill sent a team to England to make plaster casts of the stones which were then duplicated in concrete. Stones in the circular original have fallen down or are missing, but Hill restored his version. He dedicated the monument to Klickitat County men who had lost their lives in the First World War.

Origin of the genuine Stonehenge is still a mystery (the Druids being credited only by popular fancy). Hill's engineers went to great pains to place the replica so the rising sun on the morning of the summer solstice would align with the altar and the Hele stone just outside the circle. The ancient builders are supposed to have done it that way, and it is possible the arrangement of stones had some connection with calendar computations.

The Hele Stone is outside to the left, the altar to the right in the circle.

Maryhill Museum overlooks the Columbia.

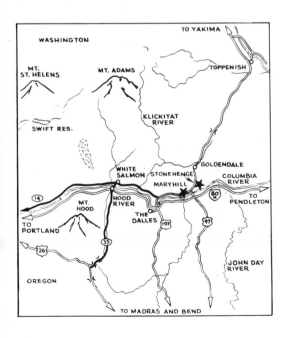

Both Stonehenges, though, are not entirely accurate sun-dials. The Portland Oregonian sent a reporter to check up on Stonehenge-west and found that the first rays of Mid-Summer's Day do not fall upon the Hele Stone with rifle-sight accuracy. The clock ran slow. The eastern horizon is a high ridge which the sun must clear. Maybe if the mountain top were bulldozed off, Sam Hill's engineers and astronomers would fare better.

The Maryhill Museum has been described as "an organized hodge-podge." It is as eccentric as its builder was, with modern art and old masters, pottery and buttons, ancient books and manuscripts, as good an Indian collection as you could hope to see and the royal accoutrements of Romania, totally out of context with the setting.

PALOUSE FALLS
It Kept Its Coulee

Although the Palouse canyon was part of the topographical remodeling caused by Ice Ages, it was not a Grand Coulee slop-over (see Dry Falls). Some geologists say the source of water was in Montana, from a gigantic lake in which Flathead is vestigial.

Flathead Lake is east of the Continental Divide. However, a lake formed there from a melting glacier could spill through even today's passes, which might have been lower a few million years ago. Traced west, the waters could have roared through Palouse canyon.

Palouse, like Dry Falls, kept cutting its way up the coulee. Dry Falls ran out of water but Palouse is still at it.

The Palouse river can claim an excellent education. It went through both Princeton and Harvard before arriving at its falls Look at the town names in Idaho, up near its source.

Considering the size of the plumbing job that makes it run, Palouse Falls has been rather slighted by sightseers. That situation is likely to change, though, when a new highway links Walla Walla and cross-state I-90 farther north. Like the Mullan Road (pages 128-129) it heads for a Snake River crossing near this point.

A 198-foot waterfall spilling out of one of the hundreds of usually bone-dry coulees was not, of course, overlooked by any explorer. David Thompson, methodically tracing the Columbia and its tributaries in 1811 in the interest of the North West Fur Company, noted its presence. Capt. John Mullan was impressed, too, when he explored his wagon route.

Palouse Falls is in a state park with campsites that overlook its gorge, but the greatest attention it has received was when it became an incidental sight for those visiting the Marmes Man diggings (pages 78-79).

Strange formations were left standing near Palouse Falls. (Right) A rough trail leads to the lower river. State park rangers warn against snakes.

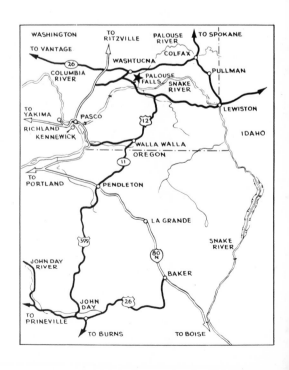

MARMES MAN
The Country's Oldest Inhabitant

The most startling archeological and anthropological discovery possible in the Western world (short of interplanetary artifacts) would be proof that man did not originate on the other side of the world, but in North or South America. Unless that happens, though, we must go along with the theory that the natives got here as Asians, by a land bridge between Siberia and Alaska before the last Ice Age ended, 14,000 years ago.

How did they spread clear to the far tip of South America and become Indians, in that short time? The walking distance from Bering Strait to Tierra del Fuego is maybe 15,000 miles. The immigrants would have to move south on the average of only five miles a year—starting in 13,000 B.C.—to have arrived at the end of the line 10,000 years ago.

The oldest of the immigrants must have settled in Alaska, but their traces were erased in the floods caused by receding glaciers. The last Ice Age covered half of what is now Washington State. Sometime between 11,000 and 13,000 years ago men were living just below the glacier line, and their campsites were not wiped out.

Countless generations may have moved on south by that time. The significance of the archeological discovery in Washington was that no northern site can be older.

Archeologists stick to modest Carbon-14 datings, mathematical recordings of their diggings, and who was there, when. "When," by their count, was not less than 11,000 years in the past, and "who" means they dug up actual human remains older than any others found in the Western Hemisphere.

This most fruitful of all American finds was drowned early in 1969 by backwaters of Monumental Dam on the Snake River. An attempt to save the site by surrounding it with a levee failed. Water seeped up from below the dike. In a last-minute wishful thinking endeavor, archeologists covered their work with plastic and protective backfills. They thought it might help scientists who continue the work a century or five centuries from now.

If you go there, a short way up the valley of the Palouse River which flows into the Snake, you will not see the Marmes site except as a cave arch appearing above water level. You can think, though, of the 15,000 years in the past and about the future when perhaps the work of interpretation of mankind's history will continue.

"Marmes Man" was named for the family that owns the ranch where the discovery was made and who helped in the development of the site.

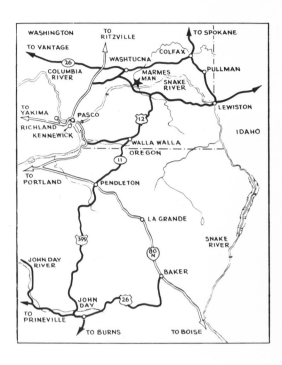

The Marmes Cave has been submerged to its ceiling, but many other caves around Palouse Canyon and in the Columbia Basin coulees were inhabited by the first humans on the continent. Rock keeps shearing off the cliffs above, stacking a wall of talus at the entrance as is shown here.

The Whitman monument stands on the skyline above the mission site. The common grave of the 14 massacre victims is at the foot of the hill. (Right) In a century, the river meandered away but the pond on the mission grounds has been restored.

WHITMAN MISSION
The Real Massacre Was of Indians

Whitman National Monument, six miles west of Walla Walla, is well established now, the old mission grounds covered with lawn, sites of buildings marked, the foundation excavations shown under glass and explanations delivered by recordings at the push of a button.

When Dr. Marcus Whitman and his wife Narcissa founded the mission in 1835 they were not pushing their beliefs on the Indians uninvited. The Flatheads and Nez Perces had asked for teachers, and a preliminary investigation indicated they meant it. Around Waiilatpu, though, many Cayuses did not share the desire for that kind of learning.

It was necessary to grow crops for self support on such a far corner of the frontier, but another reason for farming was to show the Indians they did not have to spend their lives in search of food. Whitman, helped along with an irrigation pond, built a gristmill and a blacksmith shop, too.

The mission was dedicated to Indian welfare, but the great migration over the Oregon Trail soon afterwards turned Waiilatpu into a refuge for those who limped out of the Blue Mountains in bad shape. They swung north to the mission for food, repairs and the doctor's ministrations.

The Indians watched the traffic in growing alarm. Most wagon parties moved on after recuperation, but the mission's white population had grown to 74 by 1847. That was the year the immigrants brought along a measles epidemic and the Indians, having no immunity, caught the disease.

How much the medical knowledge of 1847 helped in curing anyone is problematical. However, Dr. Whitman tried. What the Indians saw was that when he gave medicine, a white child recovered but an Indian died. They believed he was poisoning them to make way for all those settlers.

The massacre followed. The Whitmans and twelve others were killed and the mission destroyed. The survivors were held captive until ransomed by the Hudson's Bay Co.

The common grave of the victims is marked by a monument on the top of a nearby hill. The death toll was not great compared to Indian losses. The massacre became known throughout the country and Indians were killed in "retribution" for years afterward. It also led to a call for American troops from the settlers, who were Americans, and who, by so proclaiming themselves, helped shove Great Britain out of Oregon Territory.

WASHINGTON GHOST TOWNS
Gone With the Timber—or the Oysters

Pictures and stories of Western ghost towns would fill half a dozen books. In fact, they do, all of them by Lambert Florin and published by Superior. There is even a complete book, also by Florin, that consists entirely of an index to ghost towns in 14 states and British Columbia, cross-referenced to the other books.

The question can be raised, "What is a ghost town?" but that has been done, too, by the ubiquitous Florin. He puts them in several classifications and about all we can do is to expand upon his observations.

Sometimes a ghost town is so dead it is not visible at all. It has been destroyed by time, fire or later developments on the same spot. But if something of historical importance happened there, now marked only by a monument or a plaque, the ghosts live on.

In one respect, every metropolis is a ghost town because it began with a trading post or a fort long since erased. In Seattle, a plaque on a building marks one corner of the stockade that stood there during the Indian attack of 1856. And everyone knows Yesler Way was a road down which logs were skidded by ox-teams to a sawmill on the waterfront, the city's first industry.

The Skidroad area was a lively place where money was spent freely by men in from sea or logging camps, or who had returned with a bit of luck from Alaska goldrushes. Eventually the spending on drinks and entertainment moved farther uptown, leaving the oldest buildings to those who were now older, too, and broke.

The name became a generic term, often erroneously called "Skid Row," applied to rundown sections of cities all over the country. Thus that part of ghost-town Seattle was immortalized in the English language, along with "Bowery" from ghost-town New York.

A completely deserted village with buildings still standing is, of course, what most people think of. These tend to be in regions that saw mining stampedes that built towns almost overnight and left them to die just as fast.

Washington also has places that were founded on logging or the sea or both. Like the gold inland, trees ran out of ready supply and the loggers moved on. Fort Blakely once boasted the world's largest sawmill but nothing remains of it but stubs of rotted piling seen at low tide.

The long-faded-or-gone villages oriented to water were peculiar to the territory in that only Washington has a maze of saltwater channels. The channels were the sole transportation arterials before roads were hacked through evergreen jungles. The little ports all began in what seemed a strategic location for landing supplies and taking out produce or fish, but they lost their importance when roads and automobiles arrived.

The most unusual "gold rush" that petered out belonged to Oysterville on the North Beach Peninsula. Native oysters were discovered in Willapa Bay in 1851 and shipped fresh to a ready market in San Francisco. Soon there was a cannery and a smoking plant, and Oysterville thrived as the seat of Pacific County until the 1890's.

Younger South Bend took away the county seat, the oysters were depleted and finally a mysterious plague wiped out what were left. The industry was revived years later with the importation of the bigger Japanese spe-

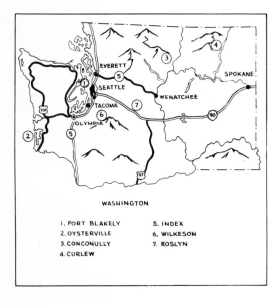

WASHINGTON

1. PORT BLAKELY   5. INDEX
2. OYSTERVILLE   6. WILKESON
3. CONCONULLY   7. ROSLYN
4. CURLEW

Ghost towns also had suburbs. This cabin is near Nighthawk.

cies and "farming" methods, so Oysterville has a wharf again and modern processing plants. The old hotels and business establishments are gone, but a number of homes in the neighborhood bear dates of a century or more in the past.

Although the label may annoy the residents, ghost towns still inhabited can be the most interesting. They tend to have prospered on mining, as did Conconully and Curlew in the Okanogan Highlands, or Index in Snohomish County, where the principal ore was copper. Coal was the business of Wilkeson in Pierce County and Roslyn north of Cle Elum.

Since towns like these were never entirely deserted, their original buildings were subject to some maintenance and less vandalism. It is easy to visualize them as they were at their peak.

Bourne was left with its main street intact. (Right) A gold dredge worked the Powder River until it came to Sumpter's city limits, where it had to quit. Sumpter was an incorporated town and there was nobody left to unincorporate it.

OREGON GHOST TOWNS
Or, On to the Next Gold Strike

Oregon's prime example of a once leading city that declined, sat dormant for years and then was "discovered" because it was still sturdy and represents a period, is Jacksonville. It was founded in 1852 and a number of its buildings are well more than a century old.

Gold started it, but Jacksonville was on the main north-south stagecoach route and was the seat of Jackson County. The "new" courthouse was constructed in 1883 and is now a very good museum. The railroad went through Medford, five miles east, so it became the county seat. However, Jacksonville's population is back to 1,500, enthusiastic about restoration.

A ghost town that came and went with a railroad is Shaniko in north-central Oregon. It is described on pages 88-89.

Number One among romantic mining towns is Canyon City, two miles south of John Day. It leaped to life in 1862 when prospectors struck it rich there. A stage route, a pony express and freight wagon trains ran to The Dalles (see Sherar's Bridge) and both Indians and bandits succumbed to temptations to intercept them enroute.

Union and Confederate sympathizers engaged in their own small battle of the Civil War on July 4, 1863. Among the town's flamboyant characters was Joaquin Miller who later became known as a poet. Others attracted attention by more direct means and the town has a Boot Hill cemetery.

Canyon City might rival the two Virginia Citys today if a 1937 fire had not destroyed much of its midtown appearance. Enough remains, though, to keep it interesting and the museum goes a long way toward making up for what is gone.

The biggest collection of mining town sites is in Baker County in the northeast, reached by going south out of Baker six miles to the Powder River, then 20 miles up it to Sumpter.

These places are described in Superior Publishing Company's series on ghost towns. Our favorite is Bourne, because many of its buildings still stand and because it ran two kinds of mining simultaneously. There was gold, all right, but the citizens kept that while they sold stock to Easterners.

There were two editions of the town's weekly, one with news for local readers and another that went East, "reporting" one strike after another to potential investors. Playing dudes for suckers was not considered cheating.

OREGON
1. JACKSONVILLE
2. CANYON CITY
3. BAKER COUNTY GHOST TOWNS

IDAHO GHOST TOWNS
Too Much for the Earps or Calamity Jane

In its early history, Idaho was transient territory. Almost everyone just passed through, starting with Lewis and Clark. After them came the fur traders but they dropped out when the profits did. Then the missionaries moved in but with one notable exception, at Cataldo Mission (page 130) they failed to influence the Indians very much and gave up.

The Mormons forged up from Utah to try agriculture in the southern part of the state. The desert defeated them and they moved away. By 1860 there was activity all over the West but Idaho's only settlements were military posts along the Oregon Trail. By that time, in fact, much of Idaho had been given back to the Indians except for road easements.

The treaties were hardly signed, though, before gold was found in 1860 in territory off-limits to whites. The U.S. Army, with no great enthusiasm for its job anyway, could not keep out the stampeders who started Lewiston, Orofino, Pierce and other towns.

It was all Washington Territory at the time, and the shift of population to the goldfields caused a political situation. Walla Walla said it was now the center of things and ought to be the capital. Through some quick connivance between Olympia and Lewiston, Idaho Territory was split off in 1863, with Lewiston as the capital. Walla Walla was left as a Washington city off in a corner.

The scene of action changed fast, though, Lewiston lost the capital to Boise as the miners spread south and east, then on to the part of Montana included in Idaho Territory. To save its hide, Boise quickly opted for the Olympia maneuver and Montana Territory was set apart in 1868.

The gold rushes created a stir in northern Idaho because of the Mullan Road (page 128) but it, too, saw through traffic, no turns. It was 1882 before strikes were made at Eagle and Murray in the northern part of Shoshone County.

Eagle has disappeared but Murray is still on the map. It once claimed a population

(Below) Precise fitting of logs was why some ghost town buildings still stand.

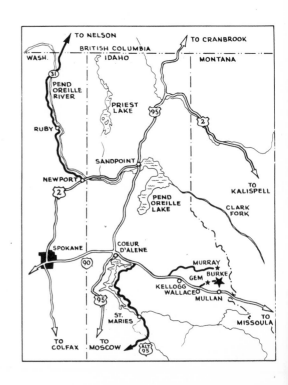

Dixie was a mining town just north of the Salmon River, mid-state.

of 10,000 and was the county seat. About 150 persons live there now, trying to preserve what is left of the town for its historical interest.

After the gunfight at the O.K. Corral in Tombstone, Wyatt Earp and two brothers, James and Warren, got out of Arizona and went to Eagle in 1884. They purchased some mining claims, and according to court records, jumped others. Wyatt also ran a saloon in a tent.

They did not fare as well as they had in Arizona. The men who went to Idaho were mostly veterans of other goldrushes and boomtowns. The Earps lasted for about nine months, quarreling over claims that did not pay off, anyway. When they left town, the assessor seized the saloon tent for nonpayment of $8.67 in taxes.

Calamity Jane, a real battleaxe by her photographs, took a look at Eagle and Murray and went back to Deadwood, S.D. She could not compete with Molly Burdan. Molly was young, and among her other qualities, was reputed to have a heart of gold—as well as a tubfull of it after she had been around Murray for a while.

She had the dramatic good sense to die at 35, at the height of her career. Molly's grave, with a wooden headmarker, is still a sentimental shrine in the Murray cemetery.

Burke, seven miles north of Wallace, rates among living ghost towns and is especially picturesque from being crowded into such a narrow canyon. Long before metropolises thought of putting high-rise buildings over freeways, Burke's main hotel spanned the railroad track. The lower lobby was for passing trains.

Not the least of this area's colorful history were the battles between unions and mining companies from 1892 to 1899. Two mines and one former governor were blown to bits in the process.

SHANIKO, OREGON
It Sure Missed the Train

U.S. 97, the main arterial east of the Cascades, sweeps past what has been called "Oregon's most interesting ghost town" with scarcely a glance at the cluster of buildings by-passed by a curve, but in the early century traffic converged on the now-leftover corner.

Shaniko was the terminus of the Columbia Southern Railway, which carried wool, sheep, cattle and wheat to Biggs, on the Columbia River, and building materials and machinery back again. It was so profitable its local builders soon cashed in by selling the line to the Union Pacific.

Before 1901 a round-trip to The Dalles took a week, and since a wagon could not haul much, nobody was prospering. As for Shaniko, it was a stage stop at August Scherneckau's ranch. Pronounce the German's last name as it might have sounded to others and you will see why it became "Shaniko."

Since Shaniko sprang up as a railhead, its streets and saloons saw their tense moments when sheepmen and cattlemen, still feuding over the ranges, arrived in town simultaneously. The railroad also speeded the advance of a third element they both hated, farmers and their barbed-wire fences. However, conflicting groups must have segregated themselves in their own saloons and other playgrounds, which were numerous, because Shaniko has no Boot Hill. It never had a cemetery or a church.

A more dignified social life was pursued at the 28-room Columbia Southern, built as soon as the railroad arrived. Wool buyers, stockmen and business entrepreneurs met there. It stands solidly today, as the Shaniko Hotel.

Shaniko was centered in a region of permanent agricultural growth so it saw no threat to its future. For ten years it was a capital of commerce and, according to some viewpoints, of sin.

Then a better graded railroad reaching farther into the state was built a few miles to the west, up the Deschutes River. At the same time a few oddballs appeared with clumsy trucks, hauling wheat between breakdowns.

From then on it was just a matter of time and highways. Shaniko kept busy for a while but its decline was hastened by the depression of the 1930's. During the Second World War 16 miles of rail between Shaniko and Kent, to the north, were removed for scrap iron. The rest of the line was pulled up in 1967.

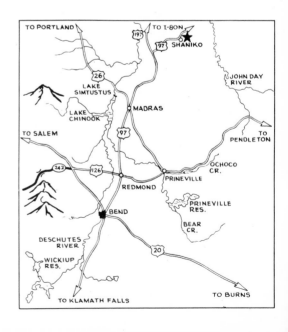

(Left)   The former saloons hold museum pieces today.   (Above)   The long-abandoned schoolhouse.   A bus now takes a few children 16 miles to classes.

Shaniko never gave up the ghost entirely. Its population dropped below 40 but it now hovers around 60, nearly half of them men who are retired or are on welfare. They live in the Shaniko hotel, at a rate that prevailed when they were young.

The remains of the town are an open museum. Many collections are the work of a Portland hobbyist. There also is a "City of Shaniko Restoration Club," but there isn't much money nor many residents of Shaniko to carry on proper preservation let alone restoration.

Former saloons contain a miscellany, most unclassified, from Shaniko's past and are open to anyone who wanders along the board sidewalk. Everything in town is worth a camera shot—wagon collection, livery stable, an old watertower that looks like a blockhouse, the long-abandoned school and the combined city hall-firehouse-jail with a firebell tower alongside.

PAINTED HILLS
In Strawberry, Vanilla and Chocolate

The first time we ventured into the Painted Hills of Oregon many years ago, we were accompanied by junior members of the family. Parents looked at the scene in disbelief. It could not be true. Whoever heard of hills that came in peppermint stripes, wintergreen bands and licorice?

The children took it in stride. They had seen such things in their preschool picture books. As a fairy tale illustration, there was nothing odd about the landscape.

You had to know where the Painted Hills were, back then, and go looking for them by turning off on a gravel road three miles west of Mitchell and driving six miles north. There you swung left through a ranch gate and forded a stream with the car.

The hills have been in an Oregon State Park all these years, but a state never kept quieter about such a remarkable attraction. It was wise of Oregon, until it could set up protection. The hills are made of volcanic popcorn and anyone who even walks from one to another leaves his footprints between. It is a delicate ecology for sure.

That makes it a challenge to motorcycle riders, who have tried to see how far up the slopes they can ride without tipping over and sliding back in the soft surfaces.

The access to the park from U.S. 26 recently has been paved. We hope it means Oregon also is ready to post rangers on the spot, preferably cold-eyed characters with a six-gun slung low on the hip, and who will meet motorbike riders in the trail and drawl, "You have until high noon to get out of here."

If you are a peaceable non-destructive explorer and are let through, do not stop with the closest vista points. Go on into the valleys beyond, even though you may have to back up when a dirt road suddenly dead-ends.

The spectacular part comes first but farther on are excellent examples of beginning erosion, revealing how the colorful hillsides were exposed to view.

(Right) Motorbike tracks.

(Left) The hills.

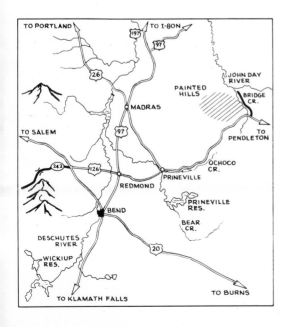

BLUE BUCKET OF GOLD
Did It Ever Exist?

It makes little difference whether there ever was a Blue Bucket of Gold. There was no Northwest Passage, either, but looking for it led to a lot of other discoveries. The same can be said of El Dorado, the Fountain of Youth and the Seven Cities of Cibola.

Not that the Blue Bucket caused equally widespread exploration. Those who went in search of the stream where the bucket supposedly was filled confined their efforts to eastern Oregon, but of course that covers a lot of territory when the object is to find something as small as a patch of gold nuggets, which are notoriously elusive.

The story became instant legend through a familiar formula, the telling and retelling of an incident that might have been true but also could have been made up by a straight-faced joker several years later. Or maybe it had a nugget of truth and grew by exaggeration as it was passed along.

Those who did find gold certainly were not on the backtrail of Meek's Cut-Off, the route allegedly used by the wagon party that first picked up nuggets they did not recognize as gold.

The Oregon Trail crossed the Snake River at Farewell Bend near Weiser, Idaho, and led northwest over the Blue Mountains and on to the Columbia. It was a circuitous route to Oregon City and Stephen Meek, brother of the more famous Joe Meek, decided in 1845 to continue straight west, to a spot that later also became known as Farewell Bend and finally Bend, on the Deschutes River.

Meek's Cut-Off turned into Meek's Disaster. The wagon train got lost on the high waterless desert and when it did reach the Deschutes, was too weak to cross the Cascades to the mid-Willamette Valley. It staggered down-river to The Dalles after all. (See Sherar's Bridge, pages 98-99).

However, the route had been pioneered and other wagon trains, forewarned and better prepared, followed the trail. Today it is called U.S. 20. Stephen Meek had a good idea but not the supplies or equipment to back it.

East of Burns, streams do cross the route and for half its distance it follows the Malheur River which flows into the Snake. The story goes that a later wagon train camped at a creek to rest and some of its men fished while there. For sinkers they pounded flat some soft pebbles they found in the gravel, and the children picked up a bucketful of the pretty little rocks.

These people were on their way to the Willamette to farm and were not interested in toting along a rockhound collection. The children's pebbles got lost or thrown away

Above and left are the "Blue Bucket" type of stream.

and, according to legend, nobody thought more about it until the California rush caused so much talk about gold. Then someone who had been with the wagon train mused, "Hmm, I wonder if that's what those yellow pebbles were?"

The response presumably was, "You wonder WHAT? WHERE?" But several years had passed and one stream or butte was not a lot different, in memory, from many others and neither was one slow plodding day from the next. The directions to the stream were that it was "over there someplace."

If the story was true, the gold must never have been found. While the searchers of the back trail were over there, though, they headed into the valleys farther north and made strikes in Baker County and at Canyon City. (See Oregon ghost towns.)

No doubt they would have gone there anyway, but all eastern Oregon discoveries are credited to the Blue Bucket. The legend was distributed as a syndicated feature.

Since it confined no one to set bounderies, you can go looking for Blue Bucket streams throughout the northeast quarter of Oregon. They may not yield any yellow metal but nevertheless many of them are treasures. Unlike streams west of the Cascades, where water already is abundant, these glitter where they can be appreciated.

Whether following or crossing the streams, persons drawn to this kind of country keep visualizing campspots for emigrants or trailriders between towns, or cowpunchers—or, wistfully, themselves.

ROCKHOUNDS PARADISE
Prineville Stakes a Claim on Itself, Too

Northwest rockhounds, or as we described them elsewhere, thunderegg nest robbers, look upon Prineville, Oregon, as the Rockhound capital of the world. Or if they don't, Prineville does.

Prineville is in Crook County, which has a Chamber of Commerce. Now, or in the past, a majority of its members must have been rockhounds. Hobbyists of that species are not always welcome on either public or private land because they burrow, looking for treasure.

In entire sympathy with the hobbyist's problem, the Prineville - Crook County Chamber of Commerce went out and staked mining claims on 1,000 acres in the vicinity. It invites rockhounds—come one, come all—to work the claims and take home what they find.

Certain restrictions are set. You can't use jackhammers, bulldozers or high explosives in working the claims, and the Chamber reserves the right to limit the amount of material taken out.

On the other hand, there are commerical rockhound claims on which the owners do kick the surface around with bulldozers to give diggers a better chance. They are charged 20 cents a pound for what they find and want to carry away.

There are 12 Prineville area claims and the Chamber of Commerce has prepared instruction sheets on how to get to each one, with tips on what may be found there. Whistler Springs, White Rock Springs and White Fir Springs are places to look for thundereggs, they say. Other spots yield green jasper, agate, dendrites, petrified wood, obsidian and good things like that.

To see what kind of diggings inspire a rockhound, we followed a perpetually curving Forest Service road beyond Stein's Pillar. It wound up a mountain and before we got done with it, we suspected it was attempting to beat Mt. Hood's altitude record. At a point that ought to have been above tree line but wasn't, we had to stop for 15 minutes to cool the radiator in the summer's 100-degree temperature.

It was a wooded mountaintop. We were in the midst of a rockhound claim. It was riddled in all directions, as if giant mountain beavers had been there, digging under every tree and stump.

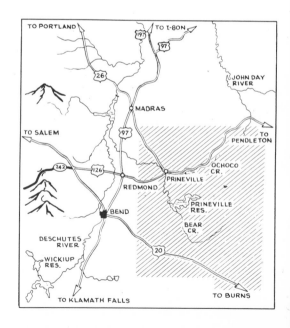

(Left) The Priday commercial fields bulldozed for rockhounds, and above, typical hunting grounds around Prineville.

We do not know what they were looking for but there would not be so many burrows unless they stood a good chance of turning up something. When the radiator cooled, we coasted down the south side of the mountain and came out on the highway to Mitchell.

Washington rockhounds seem to feel that Oregon has the happy hunting grounds but that may be due to the greener-fields syndrome, or maybe because there are fewer hunters per capita in the larger, less populated state.

Both states yield petrified wood because they had extensive lava flows that buried logs and turned them into stone by silicon replacement. When lava cooled quickly, it became glassy black obsidian.

Volcanic action also produced thundereggs, round agate deposits that were formed in gaseous cavities in lava. Rockhounds saw them in two with great anticipation of what pattern they will find inside. A thunderegg can be sterile or it may hatch a beautiful chick.

On the seacoasts of both states well polished agates and moonstones are found, and some jasper. There are Washington mining claims staked for rockhounds in the Blewett-Swuak Pass area, Redtop Mountain being best known.

Rockhounding is prospecting and therefore is accompanied by a certain reticence on the part of its most successful followers. There are books on the subject though, and state-published pamphlets that give tips on the most likely areas.

ARROWHEADS
When You Find Them You'll Get the Point

Compared to rockhounds, collectors whose main interest is Indian artifacts are few in number. They have far less chance of success even if they do more preliminary research. They tend to be secretive because if they have found a likely spot, it is similar to knowing where the X is on a buried treasure map.

Furthermore, they live under a shadow. A hobbyist who collects artifacts is a "pot hunter", or if he digs up bones, a "grave robber". When a professional does the same thing he is called an archeologist and is quick to sneer at amateurs.

In truth, amateurs have contributed a great deal to archeology when they have been intelligent and honest enough to stop their own digging and report what looks like a significant discovery to the scientists. They also have gathered many a collection on display in museums.

Arrowheads, stone tools, pestles and bowls that are found on the surface are generally legitimate prizes—unless, of course, they are taken from an area where removal is prohibited. Finding them requires a study of trade routes, camping sites and sources of the material used in the objects.

The arrowheads shown here are in the Sacajawea State Park Museum, situated where the Snake River meets the Columbia. It was a natural camping spot. Lewis and Clark and later explorers stopped here, as had Indians for centuries before. The museum's display is explanatory as well as extensive.

STEIN'S PILLAR
A Ridiculous Rock

Just beyond the Ochoco Reservoir nine miles west of Prineville, eight miles of graveled sideroad leads north to Stein's Pillar. Anyone who goes there on purpose knows beforehand what it looks like, from descriptions or pictures of it.

When he gets there, though, he still finds that Stein's Pillar is an implausible freak. The wooded Mill Creek valley up to then has normal rounded hillsides. Then suddenly this Thing sticks up above the timbered skyline.

Geologists explain it in such terms as "soluable zeolites and other minerals that have been case-hardened by rain and exposure to air." They probably mean the pillar was a particularly tough volcanic core left when all else weathered away from it.

It is 350 feet high and 120 feet in diameter. Everybody takes pictures of it as it rears incongruously against a pine forest. For a closer view, you can go a mile farther and turn right on an old C.C.C. road (Forest Service No. 1334) for 1½ miles. Take to feet for another mile to the foot of the pillar.

There are others similar to it up the valley, but they are not reached by roads.

It should have eroded away with the rest of the hillside, but it didn't.

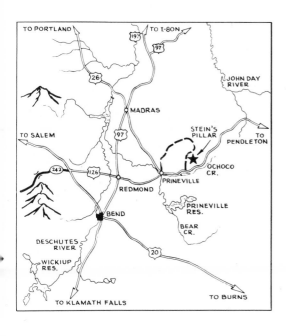

SHERAR'S BRIDGE
Travelers Bawled at the Tolls

The builders of the Barlow Toll Road and of the Naches Pass road went to prodigious efforts over a long stretch of miles to open routes to travelers. Joseph Sherar was commercially smarter. He concentrated his energies at one spot, a strategic crossing of the raging Deschutes River, and built a toll bridge there.

He didn't even have to conduct a feasibility study first. Early explorers, following established Indian trails, found a village and a narrow bridge at the site. When Sherar came along he built one for wagons and established a motel nearby. In those days they called a motel a stage station.

Sherar had it made both ways. Travelers who balked at the toll he set for using the bridge—or according to some accounts, the approach to it—could either camp out or stay at his inn while they were making

Indians fishing in the Deschutes River.

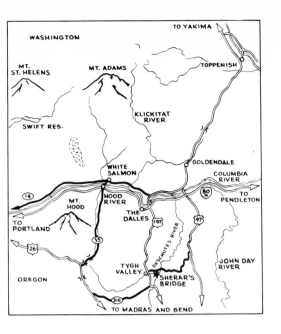

Stagecoach road near Sherar's Bridge.

up their minds whether to meet his price or go look for some other crossing.

There were no other bridges over the Deschutes, and this route led both north to The Dalles and west to Tygh Valley and the Barlow Road. In Sherar's day the heaviest traffic was between The Dalles and Canyon City far to the southeast, where gold was discovered in 1862. Stagecoaches ran between two of Oregon's largest towns.

Now, Oregon State Highway 216 crosses the bridge. Sherar did not build it and furthermore he is long gone so there is no toll.

Today's novelty in this area is ironic. It is a place to watch Indians still fishing in the rapids by the traditional and customary means that were guaranteed to them elsewhere, over and over, by treaty, but which were wiped out when a power dam was built or it suited the whims of the treaty-makers to point to the fine print in the document.

The greatest dip-net salmon fishing from platforms built over a river took place at Celilo Falls in the Columbia, but ("excuse it, please") The Dalles Dam backed up water that submerged the historic spot.

The Army Corps of Engineers has not yet come up with a workable plan to flood out Deschutes fishing with a dam, so the Indians continue their activities as they have for centuries. It is one of the few places where a treaty still means what it said and where the original scene still can be observed.

Remnants of more recent history can be found in the area by foot explorers who walk through a culvert under a railroad fill west of the bridge. The photograph on the right page was taken that way. Cut off by the fill and the new highway, it is apparently the remains of the old Dalles-Canyon City stagecoach road.

A party led by Stephen Meek, brother of the almost legendary Joseph L. Meek, came this way in 1845, seeking a shortcut to the Willamette Valley before Barlow discovered it. Some 70 members of the wagon train died before they got through, and two are buried about three miles north and west from Sherar's Bridge.

PICTURE GORGE
Kilroy and Others Were Here

The John Day River is a good example of the kind described under "Blue Bucket of Gold." It flows out of the mountains of Baker County, west through the town of John Day and north to the Columbia, passing through some of the otherwise most arid and sparsely settled country you would hope to see—or not see, depending upon your taste.

It was the route of a stage and pony express line from Canyon City to The Dalles while Canyon City was booming from a gold strike. The traffic irritated the Indians. They set fire to one stagecoach stop which still shows on the map as "Burnt Ranch". Another time they were disappointed, when they raided a stage coach, to find not much aboard but a chest of green paper issued by the U.S. Treasury. They left the paper scattered all · over the ground—litterbugs on their own land.

Downstream from the town of John Day, where the river swings northward, it went through a stretch that has interested paleon-tologists. Here evidence of an ancient land was exposed by the sharp erosion of the river. It had been damp enough for jungle that supported pre-historic animals.

This narrow cut through the strangely colored hills was a well-traveled path long before stagecoaches used it. Passing Indians had painted messages, or maybe the current school of fine art, on the canyon walls, so many that white settlers called it Picture Gorge. Some pictures remain, but most of them fell victim to modern pictographs by spray can.

Just north of the gorge is the Thomas Condon John Day Fossil Beds, a state park, but it is only a parking lot with a couple of monuments. Dr. Thomas Condon was the man who discovered the fossil beds almost as soon as the first settlers arrived.

One can look across the river, though, at the oddly shaped and colored peak on the other side and think about all those prehistoric creatures that lived below it when there was no mountain.

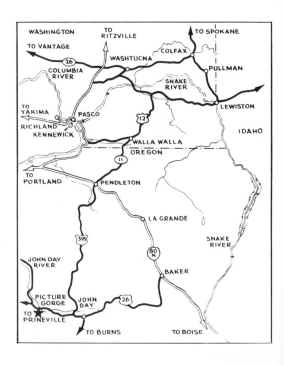

A few pictographs have not been destroyed in Picture Gorge. (Left) The John Day River and the distinctively sharp peak at the Gorge.

SMITH ROCK
A Swatch of Peaks Attracts Mountaineers

Smith Rock is singular, even though there are more than one. It is quickly apparent why it (they) was (were) put there. It was part of Oregon's policy to provide an appropriate spot for all kinds of outdoors hobbyists, whether they are wildlife watchers, myrtle-wood carvers, thunderegg nest robbers or, in this case, practicing mountaineers.

What they have in Smith Rock State Park is a miniature mountain range only two miles off a main highway. They can hike clear around it on a five-mile trail, but it also rises so perpendicularly it looks higher than its actual 500 feet above Crooked River.

Being so steep, it makes mountaineers want to climb its peaks. Being so handy, it allows a climbing expedition to be geared to a week-end. Finally, it offers challenges to every degree of skill, from beginners who are taken there for rock-work training to the real fanatics who cannot rest until the unscaleable is scaled.

The real nose-thumber as far as the fanatics are concerned is Monkey Face.

The squared-off column, 300 feet high, is not merely perpendicular, it is topped by a rocky roof with eaves. To get to its peak, a climber would have to hang supine while crawling up around an eave. Quite plainly that is impossible, so naturally it made mountaineers want to try. Somehow a party managed it in 1960, and no doubt others have turned the top corner since then.

It is better to be a photographer, happy enough with capturing the color of the cliffs, the seemingly "massive" peaks that fit into the field of an ordinary lens and views of the well-named Crooked River and its gorge, which can be taken from the encircling trail.

The usual access to the trail is not from the park campsite at the end of the Smith Rock road. Another road parallels an irrigation canal until it runs through a tunnel in one of these little mountains. The road goes farther but it is part of the trail, so the most popular place to stop and start hiking is at the tunnel.

The Crooked River runs around singular but plural Smith Rock.

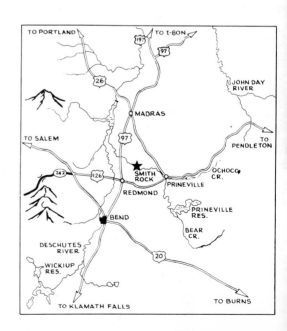

LAVA FLOW GEOLOGIC AREA
Newberry's Walls Were Like Jericho's

Oregon has a Bend in the middle and every year more people become conscious of it. The sunshine average around the calendar is two out of three days, but the middling-high altitude of the area, 3,600 feet, tempers east-of-the-Cascades heat and produces open forests. Oregon's highest peaks, five of them more than 10,000 feet, can be seen from various viewpoints. With all this and the Deschutes River, several fancy resorts for year-around activities have been built in the vicinity.

Whether it is the resorts or the Forest Service camp-grounds that draw visitors, they have plenty to look at within an hour's drive of Bend. Most of the features are geological oddities allied to volcanic action in the not-so-distant past.

Taken separately they can remain merely oddities of passing interest. The way to approach this part of Oregon, therefore, is with a comprehensive view. Then it all ties together, from McKenzie Pass to Glass Buttes, far to the east, and south to Fort Rock and Hole-in-the-Ground, off Highway 31.

Much of this region is in the Deschutes National Forest and the Forest Service has recently set up a program to interpret the whole geologic action in that manner, rather as though it were a battlefield of nature's forces. The central vantage point is Lava Butte on U.S. Highway 97, 11 miles south of Bend.

Lava Butte is of recent origin, possibly from an eruption as little as 1,500 years ago that pushed the cinder cone up 500 feet above the surrounding flatland. In geological time, 15 centuries may be a brief breather for refueling the underground tanks. With that thought in mind, the high volcanic peaks along the Cascades and no-longer-existing Mount Mazama and Mount Newberry are not such ancient history after all.

Mazama and Newberry met quite different ends. Stout-walled Mazama kept building higher, perhaps to 16,000 feet, then blew itself to bits. Nothing was left but its round foundation which now holds Crater Lake.

Newberry rose off by itself, south of Bend and Lava Butte. It was a monster volcano, 20 miles across the base and probably 10,000 feet high while it was still growing. The building inspector was lax about the foundations, though, and some inferior material went into it. Instead of rising to the top in proper volcanic cone style, lava began to leak out the bottom and through fissures miles away.

Old Newberry got hollower and hollower and finally collapsed inward. On its crater rim Paulina Peak, 7,985 feet, was left as the highest point. When volcanic action was renewed, the crater managed to puff up some small cones and a huge flow of glass-like obsidian, but most of the lava popped through on the outer slopes, creating among other things the Lava Cast Forests.

Here a flow moved slowly through green timber and congealed around standing trees and those it pushed over. It piled against the uphill side of trunks and when the level subsided, the cast was left standing, several feet above ground, higher on the upper side. Horizontal casts of logs also surfaced as the molten rock spread farther down hill.

A log left its mold.

This tree was about 3 ½ -feet in diameter.

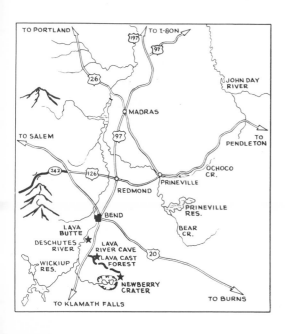

The charred wood eventually rotted away, leaving only the hollow stone stumps that had encased them above the newly-imposed surface, and a round hole down to the original ground level. Depth of the flow is therefore easily measured. It was from 10 to 20 feet.

There are several such "forests" on the flanks of Newberry Crater and probably some not yet discovered. The one opened up for visitors is in the Lava Cast Forest Geological Area, off U.S. 97 fourteen miles south of Bend, then ten miles by good Forest Service road to a campground. Stout footwear and cautious walking are necessary for getting around on the jagged surface of the old flow. Standing trees are immediately apparent but the log casts are found about a mile up the slope.

A road spirals Lava Butte to the top and the glass-walled interpretive center with a 360-degree view of the surrounding country. Parking space is somewhat limited and on holiday week-ends the popularity of the place has forced the Forest Service to control traffic from the bottom, a car up for each one that comes down.

When Newberry's volcanic activities were scattered, lava followed fault lines and surfaced at the weakest spots. Young Lava Butte began with apparent ambitions to become another Mount Hood. First cinders spewed forth from the fissure and rapidly built the cone. Next a mass of lava surged up toward the crater. If it had reached the top and spilled over, it would have set the forms in solid stone and the butte would have grown higher with each eruption.

For every volcano that makes it in a big way, hundreds poop out in the cinder stage. It was easier for the lava to break through the south wall of Lava Butte than to push its way over the brim. The mess it left as it flowed west and north is visible for miles. It plugged the Deschutes River for a while, causing it to back up a lake, fill it with sediment and return to its course over a couple of falls.

Landmarks surrounding Lava Butte are identified on dioramas. Newberry Crater's location is spotted. Charts and brochures explain what went on and where. To the west are the Three Sisters, all of volcanic origin. Just north of them is McKenzie Pass with its wild jumble of lava flows and nearby craters.

Having seen what happened on the surface, you can go underground in nearby Lava River Caves State Park and take a look at one of the conduits through which so much hot material was delivered. The park is right beside highway 97 and the

Lava Butte's top is the learning center for the whole area.

Broken Top was a volcano in the Three Sisters group.

cave is open from May through September. Visitors explore on their own and there is no entrance fee if you bring your own flashlight, which is a good precaution even if you rent a better one, a gasoline lantern, for 10 cents.

The lava tube runs under the highway and heads northwest for nearly a mile. It comes from someplace east but that section is closed. The entrance is a spot where the roof broke, exposing the tunnel which averages 35 feet in height, although there are passages little more than head-high where the trail follows the top deck of a sometimes two-story cave. The floor is sandy.

The cavern, not being a limestone cave, is not one with color and strange formations but it is fascinating nevertheless. When a lava flow crusted on the surface, molten streams continued below. If they broke out on a hillside, the fluid lava drained away and left such tubes as this one.

MCKENZIE PASS
Where the Blacktop Ran Amok

The McKenzie Pass Highway is a wagon road more than a century old whose hairpin curves are now paved. In its lower reaches east and west of the divide, it is deep in forests. At its high point it could be called "Black Pass" from the color of the savagely jagged fields of lava that extend in all directions.

The cauldrons were bubbling and overflowing here during the same periods of volcanic activity that occured around Newberry Crater and at Lava Butte on the lower plateau farther east. Geologically, both areas are so fresh they may be considered a view of what is still going on. Whether in decades or centuries, flows are quite likely to burst forth again.

McKenzie Pass and everything in sight of it bears a resemblance to the big island of Hawaii, where Kileuea and Mauna Loa are active and massive fields of lava on their slopes can be dated into this century. As for fissure eruptions around their base, those have been recent enough to be shown on TV news reports.

The Cascades' volcanic peaks, and the craters and fissures of the McKenzie area are dormant (however long "dormant" lasts) and the lava beds have been cool for slightly longer that those in Hawaii. They are so much alike, though, that the Oregon lava types have been given Hawaiian names— "aa", pronounced "ah-ah," for the sharp rough clinkers and "pahoehoe" for the smoother kind that moves in ropy or billowy flows.

The oldest lava is between 10,497-foot Mt. Jefferson and Clear Lake south of the

The Three Sisters, all over 10,000 feet, stand south of McKenzie Pass.

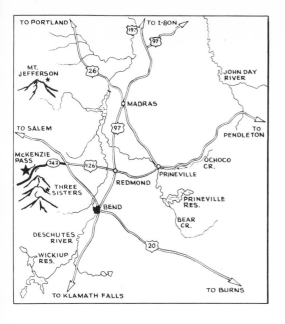

A window of the lookout tower sights on Mount Washington.

Santiam Pass highway. Through the Mt. Washington Wilderness Area to the McKenzie Pass highway, the flows date back 3,000 years or less. The wild black jumble south of the highway and down the east slope is of considerably more recent origin.

It was not the high peaks, Mt. Washington or the Three Sisters, that kicked up the fuss, it was newcomers such as Belknap Crater north of the pass, Yapoah to the south and Black Crater on the east. Like Lava Butte, they made bids to grow up and join the Big Volcano League.

They had competitors in many other cinder cones and buttes that no doubt dissipated a good deal of the energy that any one of them could muster. Belknap, for example, suffered a blowout on its east flank and developed a second dome, Little Belknap.

Yapoah poured out a molten river eight miles long and half a mile wide which ran right over what is now McKenzie Pass. It is the aa type, very uneven, with pressure ridges pushed up at the sides and a sag in the middle where the flow was fastest. The observatory is built on the top of a ridge.

Called the Dee Wright Observatory, this short round tower looks out on almost all the features involved in the volcanic action, and also at Cascade peaks clear to Mt. Hood on the north. The Three Sisters, all over 10,000 feet, are lined up to the south. Narrow windows are placed for sighting so the visitor knows what he is looking at.

Dee Wright was a packer who worked for the Forest Service from 1910 to 1934. In 1933 he was foreman of the Civilian Conservation Corps crew that built the observatory. He died before it was finished and it was named for him.

McKenzie Pass is not a route for people in a hurry nor for those in search of calendar wilderness scenes. It is for the curious. Snow lasts late and starts early and the road is not kept open. The main mid-state arterial is U.S. 20 through Santiam Pass.

FORT ROCK
Lava and Water Don't Mix

All the fuming and hot fountains of the Newberry area and McKenzie Pass was old stuff on the plains of central Oregon. Their lava-bed foundations had been laid down even before there was a Cascade Range. A vast part of the region was, in fact, under water.

The Cascades began to cut off rainfall from the west but on the other hand the mountains filled with glaciers under the influence of Ice Age frontiers that advanced and retreated not far to the north, and the runoffs helped keep the lake in existence.

Still, with conditions always changing in the north and west, the lake level was not constant. Waterfront property during one age was flooded throughout the next or it was without a drop in sight.

During a time of low water, a volcano started up on the plain. It was hot inside, perhaps in a dormant interlude, when the water slowly rose around it. The wide lake kicked up storms and waves battered at crater walls, leaving erosion marks that still can be seen.

Eventually the old volcano developed a disastrous leak. Water on molten rock built up a head of steam and the explosion destroyed the labor of centuries. Nothing was left but a basaltic crescent, 325 feet at its highest point.

Its shape made early settlers think of a fort, so they named it Fort Rock and someone obligingly made up a story of a wagon train beseiged there. Maybe so, but it is now a state park and no mention is made of such an incident in actual history.

A few miles away is an oddity called simply "Hole in the Ground" which probably was caused by similar conditions. For years it was thought to be a meteor crater, round, some 425 feet deep, and taking in a quarter-square mile.

Today's theory is that water reached hot magma far underground to form steam, and the result was equal to a major nuclear explosion. It could have happened while Mount Newberry, not too far away, was building.

That would put the explosion within sight and sound of human inhabitants. They left their sandals in a cave near Fort Rock at least 9,000 years ago, maybe because they took off in a frantic rush. (Their early ancestors could have come down south from the Marmes site.)

The crater shows, open to the plain. (Opposite) Waves of the ancient lake dashed against this wall.

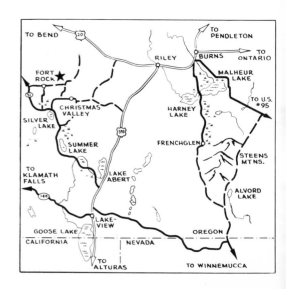

CHRISTMAS VALLEY
Real Estate Subject to a Sandy Clause

The desert country of Christmas Valley suggests anything but Christmas, and the name apparently was a cartographer's mistake. Lieut. John C. Fremont, exploring down from The Dalles, was camped farther south on Christmas Day, 1846, at Hart Lake in the Warner Valley. He called that lake Christmas but maps 60 years later attached it to the small one up north. Hart was derived from a nearby ranch whose brand was heart-shaped.

The great lake bottom, which extends north of Fort Rock, was settled by hopefuls who were defeated by the arid climate and eventually gave up. Today's Christmas Valley settlement is entirely the result of a real estate promotion.

It is Oregon's attempt at a Palm Springs, with a man-made lake, a golf course and a resort. The desert wastes for miles around have been platted in lots, many of which have been sold to Californians—perhaps smart Californians, if they remember what happened at Palm Springs.

Christmas Valley is rife with attractions, all reached by roads primitive enough that each five miles seems like fifteen.

Out east of the settlement and slightly north, 14 miles, is dry Fossil Lake. You are not likely to dig up any extinct species of birds or animals there, but paleontologists did. It is the best place to visualize the lakes that once covered eastern Oregon.

Ten miles on beyond, on a dirt road, is a fine area of sand dunes. They represent Oregon's Sahara, moving where they wish and changing contour year by year. A movie company, filming a Sahara scene, once thought they ought to have an oasis and drilled a well at their foot. It still flows from a faucet at the edge of the dunes.

From the top of the sand hills another oddity, the Lost Forest, is in sight seven miles to the northeast. Some 9,000 acres are covered by a very old stand of Ponderosa pine where pine ought not to grow. Apparently this is a surviving patch from a period when forests lined the long-gone lake.

Sand drifting among the trees would appear to be spelling their doom but actually it is the probable explanation for their survival. It prevents ground vegetation from competing for moisture, and holds down evaporation.

Sand shifts but brush is adaptable.

(Left) Dunes freshly pitted by rain.

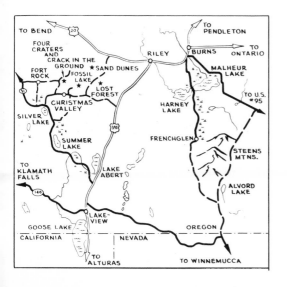

Claustrophobiacs avoid going to the bottom of Crack-in-the-Ground, but our fearless photographer (who also explores caves) shot a picture skyward from the floor of this odd fracture in the earth.

The sand also keeps alive a story of lost gold. A cowboy left a rock for assay, saying he had found it in or near the Lost Forest. He never came back, and of course the rock was rich in gold. Searchers have snooped through and around the forest, with the tantalizing thought that what the dunes may have covered they might uncover again.

North from the townsite of Christmas Valley, eight miles, a geological construction job was begun and abandoned. Or anyway, there has been no progress for the past 1,000 years. It could have been planned as another fault escarpment like Abert Rim to the southeast.

The crack in the basaltic surface was opened for a couple of miles and outlined for several miles more on each end, as can be seen from the air. The open section is 10 to 15 feet wide and as deep as 70 feet in some places. At that stage little further development went on, either in lateral or up-and-down movement.

However, the effort was not entirely wasted. Later on, four craters took advantage of the crack to bring their lava to the surface. They are strung out for three miles along the line to the north. One of them sealed a section of the fissure with its flow, which helped geologists date the happenings.

Fort Rock Valley to the northeast (page 110) is a bay of this big basin. The Four Craters are recent enough to have been formed about the same time Lava Butte and its surrounding volcanic activity was going on (pages 104-107).

In between is Newberry Crater, the source of numerous lava flows even after it had collapsed. Around its perimeter lava caves of various kinds were formed. The one near Lava Butte has been described. Others are noted for having ice in them all year around. And on the east there is a cave with "lavacicles" instead of icicles.

As in the case of the Lava River Cave, the surface hardened while a molten stream flowed on below, broke out and drained away leaving a tube. Lavacicle Cave was sealed before it cooled, though, and lava kept dripping to form stalactites and stalagmites.

These caves are in the national forest northwest of Christmas Valley and are best approached from U.S. 97 or U.S. 20 out of Bend. The roads are graveled or dirt. The shortcut between Christmas Valley and Fort Rock is okay.

GLASS BUTTES
So Far, Unrecycled

If the Indians had gone on using arrows and spears for another millenium, they still would not have made much of a dent in Glass Buttes, 27 miles west of Riley on the south side of U.S. Highway 20. They rise 2,000 feet above the plain, one of the largest obsidian outcroppings in the world.

Glass Buttes was a mine for the material, hard and sharp for points, skin scrapers and cutting tools, but easily shaped. On top of that, the obsidian is unusually pretty. It is slightly irridescent and appears not only in jet black but in varied colors.

With qualities like that and a limitless supply, arrow- and spearheads from Glass Buttes spread far across the country. Some found in Ohio were identified as coming from Oregon.

The buttes stand like a northeast corner-post of Lake County and Christmas Valley. There is a road past but not to them. However, anyone curious about the obsidian has no trouble finding pieces. They are mixed in with the dirt along the highway.

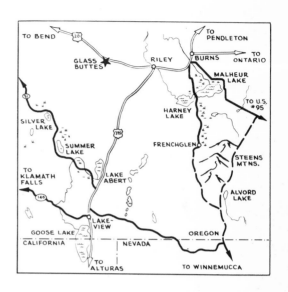

Who would guess they are glass?

STEENS MOUNTAINS
Another of Oregon's Big Faults

The allure of the Steens Mountains is their brooding solitude in a vast surrounding country little changed since the first settlers arrived. Few ever arrived and it is still many miles between villages or ranches.

Southeast Oregon has its faults and they are big ones. When the earth's crust buckled in these parts, it was on a colossal scale. Between Burns and Malheur Lake, the highway climbs over a 25-mile wall only a few hundred feet wide at the top (from which there is a view of the Steens Mountains and everything else, all directions). This was a double fault, with the crust sinking on both sides.

The Abert Rim, 25 miles north of Lakeview, is the longest exposed fault, some 30 miles, on the continent. The fracture shows 2,000 vertical feet of the old crust.

The Steens' Mountains are called the world's largest "block fault," which means something to geologists. What happened here, probably, was that when the surface broke along the fault line, some of it sank and the rest was pushed even higher. There is a 5,000-foot drop between the tallest point in Steens Mountains and the floor of the Alvord Desert below.

A few million years after all this happened and explorers came along, they were inclined to report that the country was not good for much. It was most inhospitable for domestic types that wanted to start a farm or a city.

It appeared to be ready-made, though, for those who wanted a lot that took in at least 25 square miles and the cattle men moved in. Pete French was not the biggest of them, but he was the most colorful.

Some, like John Devine, had as large a spread. William Hanley who owned the Double O and the Bell A, both between Burns and Malheur Lake, was an intellectual and an early-day conservationist.

Steens Mountains (left) are flanked on the southeast by the desolate Alvord Desert (right).

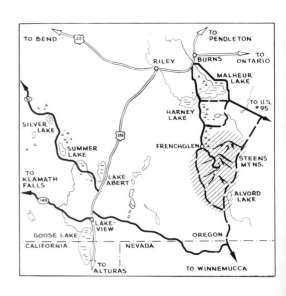

116

In the Steens, the road (left) is a highway. The sod hut (above) was a type built by pioneers.

Pete French stole the show through the belligerence of the kind established by today's TV Western programs. His cowpunchers rode armed and brooked no interference from Indians, dirt farmers or sheepmen. He had brushes with them all, and finally it was a farmer who shot him in 1897.

The jury quickly acquitted the killer. Most of French's headquarters ranch ended up, by a 1935 purchase, in the hands of the federal government for the Malheur Bird Refuge.

At the south end of the Refuge is Frenchglen, a tiny village with a tiny but interesting hotel. The place draws its name from the combination of French plus a partner who backed him with money, Hugh Glenn.

A gravel road runs east, little more than a mile, to what was Pete French's ranch house. The only things left of the original scene are the tall cottonwoods in a rectangle around the site and a barn. The rest of the place has been taken over by the bird refuge administration.

You can drive south either by the dirt road through the Malheur Bird Refuge or by paved Oregon Highway 205, slightly to the west. The dirt road can give you moments of panic but it gets to Frenchglen and is the more interesting of the two routes. (See Malheur Bird Refuge, following.)

The road south from Frenchglen is black-topped for several miles, then it ends in a dirt road that goes on forever, over the south end of Steens Mountains, finally to emerge at Fields, a small junction where a road runs north around the east side of the Steens Mountains, 131 miles to Burns—62 miles of it on gravel.

The other exit is south to Denio Junction, Nevada, then 120 miles west to Lakeview, Oregon. There is one service station in that distance, at Adel.

If you are finding your way around this country by service station map, check its date and the publisher. The H. M. Gousha Company is more likely to be correct than some others. Road conditions change from year to year—fortunately for the better, but if you have a low-slung car it is better not to count on roads marked "dirt" or even "gravel".

Only one dirt road penetrates the Steens Mountains themselves. It climbs 3,000 feet to Fish Lake. The rest of the exploration must be done on foot or by horse. Around the base of the mountains are some of the historically biggest cattle spreads of the West.

The eight-room hotel is Frenchglen's leading establishment.

Antelope are found in both the Malheur Wildlife Refuge
and in their own Hart Mountain Refuge. Not having a telephoto
lens to look through, this one didn't know how close it was
to the photographer.

MALHEUR REFUGE
Oregon's Largest Poultry Yard

When the Malheur National Wildlife Refuge was established by President Theodore Roosevelt in 1908, it took in much of the Pete French ranch and part of William Hanley's. By that time French was dead and Hanley was in accord.

This part of Oregon is an incongruity, lakes and swamps in otherwise desert country. The same thing is true of much of the southeastern part of the state, where vestigial lakes or their beds remain from prehistoric times, when the region was submerged.

The country from Burns south is desert, but for many square miles it is also a swamp. It is alternately sagebrush and sand for as far as you can see, and a damp expanse on which dirt roads run as a dike, all the way from the Malheur Lake to Frenchglen.

The lakes are huge or small, depending on the weather each season, as they have back to the Ice Age. In Southeast Oregon, lakes are marked on the map as "tentative" to this day.

Big Malheur and Harney Lakes are comparatively dependable. Malheur is the center of the wildlife refuge because it is fed by a couple of rivers, the Silvies and more importantly, the Donner and Blitzen, named when a troop of soldiers crossed it during a thunder and lightning storm and gave it a German name, just for fun.

North or southbound birds have stopped here for centuries (unlike those that discovered a new landing field at Moses Lake-O'Sullivan Reservoir, also in this book). Ornithologists have counted 248 species at the site, plus 51 species of animals that have dropped by for a drink.

They call it a "wildlife refuge" but it is just as much a refuge for birdwatchers. Everything is stuffed and labeled in the museum, and out on the nearest pond there is a blind for photographers who want to shoot pictures of the real birds floating there.

A short distance from the headquarters is a tall tower on a low hill. It is a steel framework, it sways in the wind and climbing it is not recommended to anyone with acrophobia. If skeletal heights do not bother you, the tower gives a view of an otherwise flat basin, its lakes and the swamps that attract birds.

Wandering around the hill are antelope. They seem to figure that people came there to watch birds, and since they are not birds, they should be exempt from undue scrutiny.

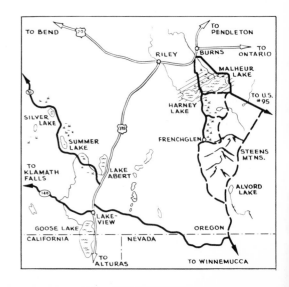

Pete French ditched and drained swampland to turn it into range or hayfields. Waterfowl enjoy today's canals.

You can return from the Malheur head-quarters to the main paved highway (Oregon 205) running south to Frenchglen, or you can drive through the reserve on its dirt roads—a slow but interesting trip.

To the north are the hills you came over. To the south and east are the Steens Mountains, uninhabited and not very hospitable. To the west are the Jackass Mountains, and beyond them a great expanse of desert. Frenchglen has a population of 20, but it is on a paved road and it seems almost like a metropolis when you arrive.

The Malheur National Wildlife Refuge takes in 180,850 acres in a long stretch from the north boundary of Malheur Lake to French-glen, with jogs off into seemingly intermin-able flats to the east.

It harbors trumpeter swans, mallards, Canada geese and ducks of all breeds, along with sage grouse, quail, partridges, chukar and pheasants. Hunters are allowed to take upland birds and some waterfowl, in the fall, in limited areas, even though it is a game reserve. There are millions of birds, which allows for some harvesting.

For visitors who just want to look, Sports Fisheries and Wildlife at Refuge headquarters furnishes check-off lists to birdwatchers and also to youngsters. Children get a pamphlet with the pictures of anything they may see in the way of birds and animals so they can identify them.

Pelicans fly above Warner Valley.

HART MOUNTAIN
Where the Pelican and the Antelope Play

The "official highway map" put out by the Oregon State Highway Division shows a road across the Catlow Valley, a shortcut between the Malheur National Wildlife Refuge and the Hart Mountain Antelope Refuge that would save 100 miles over the long way around. It is designated as "unimproved," a mild description for its actual condition midway through.

Modern machinery can make quick improvements in graveled roads across sagebrush land, but until a motorist has convinc-ing evidence that this one has been changed he should not attempt it in an ordinary passenger car.

So State Highway 140, emerging from Warner's Canyon to join U.S. 395 five miles north of Lakeview, is the route to take to the Hart Mountain Antelope Refuge. Sixteen miles east a black-topped road runs 19 miles to Plush, the remaining crossroads of a once-livelier center. Farther east a graveled road out of Adel makes it to Plush in 18 miles.

The west side of the 240,000-acre refuge

is bordered by Warner Valley lakes that vary in size by the season. The graveled road to headquarters is 24 miles long, half the distance climbing the mountain.

Hart Mountain, 7,710 feet, is the one first seen but, although it gives its name to the area, it is not the highest point. Warner Peak just to the north is 8,065 feet. Like the Steens Mountains and Abert Rim, this mass rearing more than 3,000 feet above the valley is a fault escarpment.

Pronghorn antelopes, native to North America, once roamed by the millions from Canada to Mexico and from Iowa to Eastern Washington and Oregon. By 1925 there were not more than 26,000 left.

State efforts to save them were not very effective. Laws and enforcement varied and antelopes pay no attention to state lines. In 1932 they were given three federal reservations, refuges here and in Nevada, and the Charles Sheldon Antelope Range, also in Nevada. Highway 140 passes through the Range for 34 miles after crossing the state line on the way to Denio.

The refuges were chosen because they include favorite fawning grounds. In the winter most of the antelope stay on the Sheldon Range. They wander far in the summer but many come to Hart Mountain to bear fawns and also because it has a permanent water supply when ponds elsewhere have dried up.

Rangers estimate that perhaps 200 antelope are resident, with another 500 coming and going. What with refuges, legal protection and transplants to other areas, there now may be 300,000 antelope in the Western states. They do not live to great age—eight or nine years—but fawns usually arrive as twins.

At the age of three or four days they can outrun a man, and in a week can leave a dog behind. An adult antelope's cruising speed is around 30 miles an hour but when it is in a real hurry, it can do 50.

While the antelope is the leaseholder and featured creature at Hart Mountain, their appearance is not guaranteed. However, they share the refuge with many other tenants, the rarest being a group of California Bighorn sheep. These are most likely to be spotted by hikers on the high ridges. As for mule deer, they are as numerous as the antelope.

Some 20 miles of dirt road can be driven in a tour guided by a mimeographed map and interpretations of fauna, flora and views enroute. There is one small campgrounds with a hot springs bath.

The lakes and swamps of the Warner Valley are a good place to see waterfowl, among which the most interesting are pelicans.

Lake County touts itself to rockhounds and the Chamber of Commerce in Lakeview has a map showing where to find obsidian, sunstones, fossils, uranium, cinnabar, agates, petrified wood, jasper, thunder eggs, opal and even arrowheads. The Hart Mountain refuge allows no digging but visitors can pick up and take away up to seven pounds of rock specimens.

All this is high country in which Lakeview, "down" in a valley, has an elevation of 4,800 feet. It can snow in early spring, and we were caught in a blizzard in late September.

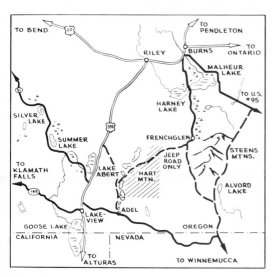

Hart Lake, with pelicans. The face of Hart Mountain rises above.

COVERED CROSSINGS
Lane County's Bridge Game

Why Lane County, Oregon, should have become a nesting ground for covered bridges is not readily apparent. One might conjecture that some newcomer from Pennsylvania, New England or Georgia moved west and built the first one, thus leading the mid-Willamette Valley residents to think all bridges should look like that.

However, that guess would be wrong. Oregon was long settled before Lane County's first covered bridge appeared. The Mosby Creek Bridge, on Lang Road four miles east of Cottage Grove, is the "antique" among two dozen of them. It dates to 1920.

A common explanation of covered bridges is that roof and siding furnished a practical protection of the timbers (and the travelers) from the weather. It is no rainier in Lane County, though, than in the rest of the Willamette Valley. One also wonders, if weather is that damaging to bridges, what was to protect the roof and sidings? As for travelers, the time they spend crossing bridges would not keep them dry for long.

Covered bridges are always associated with horse-and-buggy days. Horses were said to be less nervous when they could see neither the river nor the height at which they were crossing it. However, Oregon's bridges echoed to little clip-clopping of hoofs. Half of them were built from 1930 on—the latest in 1966.

No, the only way it can be explained is that a Covered Bridge Rennaissance broke out in Lane County after such structures were falling to pieces or were being preserved for history's sake in the rest of the country. They are scarce enough elsewhere that their fans belong to associations and list their prize relics in "World Guide on Covered Bridges."

Covered bridges were not an American design. They go back centuries in Europe and Asia and the first one erected in the United States was in Pennsylvania in 1804. They did evolve quite a bit in this country, though, during the next forty years, to the delight of today's bridge connoisseurs who note and compare one construction method with another.

Lane is an unusual county. It stretches from the Cascades divide to the Pacific Ocean, with Eugene as the county seat. The only other Oregon county approaching such a span is Douglas, just to the south, which takes in a few miles of seacoast and the west side of Crater Lake.

Covered bridges can be found in Lane County from the foot of the mountains almost to the ocean. The biggest cluster is east of Cottage Grove. The two most often seen and photographed are Goodpasture (they all have names) a mile west of Vida on the McKenzie Highway, and Belknap on the same highway downriver from McKenzie Bridge.

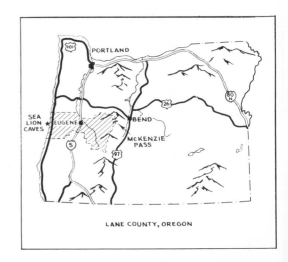

LANE COUNTY, OREGON

Currin Bridge is on Lang Road four miles east of Cottage Grove. It dates to 1924. Nearby is Mosby Creek Bridge, the oldest one, built in 1920.

MULLAN ROAD
It Was U.S. Interterritorial No. 1

To Captain John Mullan and his road-building soldiers the scene on the opposite page, near Palouse Falls, must have been beautiful. No mountains to climb, no trees to hack down, no rivers to bridge as they had been doing for five years and nearly 600 miles since leaving Fort Benton, Montana, in 1858. They still had the Snake River, to cross on the way to Walla Walla 50 miles farther, but a ferry was waiting.

Mullan, an Army engineer, pushed through the first federally-assisted highway in Washington, Idaho or Montana. The government spent $230,000, with the equivalent of matching funds in those days being that those using the road would maintain it. They didn't, of course.

"Interterritorial Highway 1" began at Fort Benton because it was the head of navigation on the Missouri River. Travel west from there was two- and four-footed. The Indian wars of the 1850's spurred the federal decision to link Fort Benton with Walla Walla by a military road.

Mullan's builders were off to an easy start on the open plains. Their first really hard work came in crossing the Continental Divide. The first two winters were spent holed up near Missoula and in the Bitterroot Mountains, with temperatures down to 42 below zero.

While I-90 does not go through the same Bitterroots pass the Mullan Road did, driving it gives one a look at the terrain. In today's highway construction, massive bulldozers are chewing additional lanes into mountainsides. Think of Mullan's men, equipped with axes, picks, shovels, black powder and horse-drawn scrapers.

The road followed down the valley and the builders celebrated Independence Day at Fourth of July Canyon, where one of them carved his initials and the date on a tree

whose stump still remains. From Lake Couer d'Alene, Mullan headed to Spokane, which had not yet been founded, and turned south at that point.

They stayed west of the Palouse River, passing within sight of the falls, until the Palouse ended in the Snake. There the cable-operated Lyons Ferry had been running since 1859, expecting Mullan to come along any year.

It continued to run until the late 1960's when the old Vantage bridge across the Columbia was reassembled to span the Snake. Mullan, who kept a journal of A.A.A.-type hints for travelers, estimated driving time for the 624 miles at 47 to 55 days. He noted the ferry charge was $4 for wagons and 50 cents for passengers.

No sooner was it opened than the "military" road became a busy arterial for miners and supplies moving to the Montana goldfields. When the rushes were over, the rutted unrepaired road became little more than a pack trail.

Captain Mullan and his crew were virtually home free when they got to this open country near Palouse Falls. If wagon drivers did not like Mullan's set of tracks, they made their own new ones.

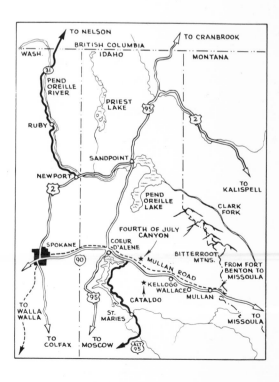

CATALDO MISSION
It Was More Than Idaho's Oldest Building

Everywhere travelers go in the world they are steered to cathedrals, churches, temples, mosques or other shrines of various religions, to look at buildings noted for their size, architectural beauty, interior decoration, antiquity or historical significance. Even in the West California has its chain of missions and Alaska its Russian Orthodox churches.

No matter how many you have visited, though, the Cataldo Mission of the Sacred Heart is worth more than the passing glance it normally gets from motorists going through northern Idaho on Interstate 90.

It is the oldest building in Idaho but that doesn't make it ancient. Indians under Jesuit instruction began building it about 1846. It was designed in classic proportions by a priest who had had architectural training, and the Indian workmen put it together with loving care.

The method of its construction may be seen in a room in back of the altar. Woven willow branches—"wattles"—were mixed with clay to form the walls which were then covered with plaster in which handprints are still visible. Beams and columns were hand-hewn from single logs and all nails were made of wood.

While this was going on the Whitmans were killed by Indians and their mission, established in 1836, was destroyed. Soon after Cataldo was finished tribes were on the warpath throughout the Northwest but the mission remained a peaceful eddy.

The Jesuits had approached the Indians in a different manner, enlisting their aid. They also were lucky enough not to be surrounded by miners and settlers killing off the game and taking away the land. By the time that happened in northern Idaho the Indians had little strength left.

They were the congregation and when they were moved to reservations, the mission fell into disuse except for an annual mass that brought them back from long distances. Caltaldo was restored in 1930 and is designated a national historic memorial.

(Left) Thanks to a priest who had studied architecture, the building had "classic" lines. (Below) Remarkable paintings were made with vegetable dyes.

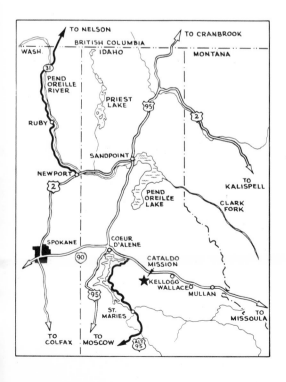

ST. JOE RIVER
It Never Knew When It Was Licked

Early in the century a dam was built in the Spokane River at Post Falls, on the Idaho side of the line between Spokane and Coeur d'Alene. It raised the level of Lake Coeur d'Alene, not drastically but enough to increase its length to 25 miles and its shoreline to about 125 miles, what with the coves created in side valleys.

The St. Joe River flows into the upper or southern end of the lake. When the lake level was raised, the water backed into the St. Joe's valley, shortening the river by several miles. Or at least that is what everyone thought had happened.

The St. Joe stubbornly refused to be curtailed. It continued on its accustomed route, lake or no lake. It went on meandering as it had before. Trees and brush along its submerged banks remained loyal. If the river ignored the change, so would they.

They were supposed to die, of course, within a few years of inundation, but there they still grow, outlining the St. Joe's channel. Thus, the "Shadowy St. Joe," as this part of the river is called, is doubly an oddity.

St. Maries (pronounced Marys) is several miles up the river but only 29 feet higher than the city of Coeur d'Alene. Boats easily cruise between the two places, using the Shadowy channel—a strange passage simultaneously a tree-lined river and, as anyone can see through its swampy "banks", a lake at the same level.

The St. Joe starts at the summit of the Bitterroots Mountains, between Idaho and Montana, but it makes no great fuss about it. For 22 miles above St. Maries it is navigable to small boats. Then it goes on and on, still at low level, almost to the Continental Divide before it becomes steep in its final few miles.

On both sides of the river Forest Service roads tap the side country every few miles, but it seems that no matter how far you drive on them, all they do is go over one ridge after another to a view of more timber over the farthest horizon.

The Continental Divide sounds impressive but it has passes all through it. Whereas Washington's mountains are punctured by only five passes, including the one in the North Cascades, there are eleven crossings of the Bitterroots in the same distance. The St. Joe River road gives you a couple of choices of going on into Montana, or if you like to live dangerously, a couple of northbound loops over the mountains into Wallace.

Don't try to make any progress up the St. Joe River if you have along a fisherman with a legal license. He will keep crying, "Stop!" on the theory that he has spotted a hole where trout lurk. He does not have to be very smart to be right.

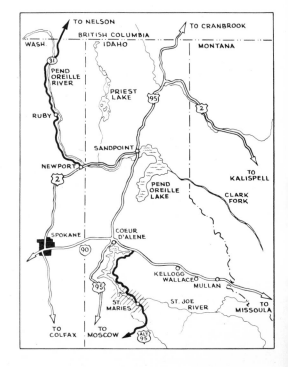

Old Man River St. Joe rolls on, ignoring the lake and sticking to its own riverbanks.

HELL'S CANYON OF THE SNAKE
The Colorado's Grand Canyon Is Shallower

As the Snake River flowed westward through Idaho, covered wagons followed its relatively easy arc until they came to what is now the border of Oregon. There the Snake ridded itself of company. Turning north at Farewell Bend, it rampaged through a gorge more than a mile deep and so unnavigable the pioneers named it "Hell's Canyon."

Hell's Canyon it remains, even in these days of high-horsepower boats. Nobody ever ran it the whole way upriver, and many who tried the stunt downriver bashed up in the rapids.

Dams at the upper end of the gorge now cut off passage clear through. Below, where the gorge is deeper than that of the Colorado's Grand Canyon, the country is still wild.

It is approached from Lewiston, Idaho, where boat trips started a century ago. Sternwheel steamers rammed and winched their way as far as they could, to unload supplies for gold seekers and the later homesteaders who had no other road to their isolated ranches.

The steamboats disappeared in the 1930's but a gasoline-powered boat continued a weekly run with mail and supplies, crashing through more than 100 sets of rapids.

Floyd Harvey, a Lewiston businessman who runs Hell's Canyon Excursions because he loves the river, depends upon modern jet boats. The mailboat still takes passengers, and a couple of Lewiston guides offer charter excursions for camping and fishing, but Harvey's operation grew up especially for tourists and is complete from end to end.

His boat leaves Lewiston early in the morning for Willow Creek, a camp he built 93 miles up the river. At Johnson Bar, four miles farther, the Snake stops all but stunt drivers willing to risk their lives trying to climb rapids that are actually low falls.

For the first 20 miles out of Lewiston, the Snake is wide and flows between the low, brown hills of Idaho on the east and Washington on the west, as far as the Grande Rone River, where the hills grow higher and the Oregon border soon is passed on the right.

The river has kicked up an "eddy" here and there. Now, rounding a corner, the jet boat charges through a wildly foaming rapids. Knowing the major rapids have been named, a passenger inquires (when his teeth stop rattling), "Which one was that?"

The pilot, relaxed on his seat, thinks for a while. "There are so many," he apologizes, "I can't remember all the little ones."

"Suicide Point" was the name given to this spot only for its potential.

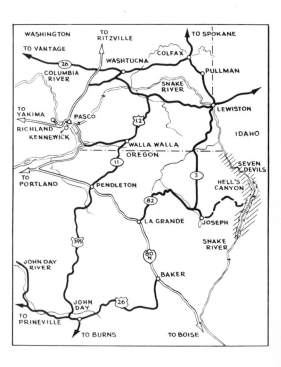

Running one of the many rapids in the Snake River.

When he gets to the big ones, the pilot unrelaxes. Standing, he drives the boat straight at one bank, cuts within six feet of a jagged boulder and whirls the wheel. The boat skitters on a diagonal course across the leaping water. Just as suddenly he reverses direction. The river is being climbed by the switchback method.

River pilots used to memorize all the rapids and their channels, and rememorize them with each seasonal change. Now, at least, they have target boards on the shore. By lining up two of them like gunsights, they can put the boat on a "recommended" course. (No rebate if a big submerged rock has rolled into the channel.)

The scenery grows more impressive, more towering with each mile. Periodically the canyon relents and falls back to allow a bench on which some pioneer staked his future to raise cattle or sheep, or to prospect. In the lower canyon, ranches may have a primitive road bulldozed to them from the far side of the mountains, but some still depend on the river as the only way in or out.

The "ports" along the river are bits of sandy beach into which a boat can ram its bow and back off again after mail, cargo or passengers are put ashore. Harvey makes periodic rest stops, including one for a box lunch, at points of interest such as a mine, rocks inscribed with Indian heiroglyphs, a proposed damsite or the place where Chief Joseph and his people crossed the river in 1877 while escaping American troops.

Above Pittsburgh Landing the feeling of wilderness increases. The mountains on both sides now rise a mile over the river. Each stream they discharge into the Snake sets up a conflict of currents and more rapids to negotiate.

At full power the boat can average about 10 miles an hour, but a sense of exhilerating speed is given by the opposite rush of water. It is almost disillusioning to learn that no excursion ever has had a serious accident, and that natives familiar with the river have jumped in, wearing a lifebelt, to bob down a rapids personally.

Nevertheless the river demands a combination of caution, a dependable motor and the pilot's knowledge of the channels. It keeps the trip adventuresome, but leaves it open to whole families.

Willow Creek, reached in late afternoon, is sheltered behind a cliff on the Idaho side, and in this nearly desert country is distinguished by a grove of pines. A sandy beach, rare in its length, extends several hundred yards. Since summer temperatures can go well over 100 degrees in the rocky canyon, no fancy resort pool furnishes more fun for the children than the dunking-shallows of the cool river.

A Forest Service trail on the mountainside invites exploration. The beach invites doing nothing. But then there are fish to catch, including that strange monster, the prehistoric sturgeon.

A freshwater Northwest sturgeon's size seems to be determined only by its food supply and how long it lives. The Snake River, and the Columbia into which it flows, once yielded sturgeon 12 to 15 feet long and weighing half a ton, but they were fished out and a ten-footer now is considered large. Three feet is under legal limit, and those longer than six feet must be thrown back to help preserve the species.

Before sturgeon were protected, river residents herded them to market. The fish were too big to drag into a boat, but so sluggish they could be tethered alive. The fishermen would catch half a dozen, six to ten feet long, then lead them down to Lewiston where they were thrown on a truck and hauled to Portland.

You can stay at Willow Creek as long as you wish, but the usual excursion returns to Lewiston after lunch the next day. Whooping downriver with the current, the trip takes only three hours. The new thrills are rapids that look like the rim of a falls—until you hurtle over the edge at 30 miles an hour. It makes for a rough ride, but by now everybody is a veteran riverboater.

The canyon would be dammed at the lower end if public and private power interests had not got into such a squabble the United States Supreme Court finally threw out the case and ordered everybody to start over.

Now, though, conservationists are speaking in a powerful voice. They oppose any dam that changes Hell's Canyon. It is too valuable to lose as a wilderness asset.

Willow Creek Camp. Floyd Harvey keeps improving it.

HOMESTEADS IN THE WILDERNESS

The West has its vast uninhabited spaces, wilderness whether it consists of mountains, desert or roadless seacoast, and many people now seek wilderness as a relief from urban pressures.

It was sought in earlier days, too. Anyone who explores these areas is periodically surprised—and even a little awestruck when he thinks of the labor involved—to find the remains of homesteads. Someone always pushed on a little farther, as a family or as a man who preferred his own company.

They settled there to stay. The defeat that left the home abondoned could have been drouth, or lack of transportation after everyone else was moving about swiftly, but it could have been simple and inevitable age.

Lars Ahlstrom is mentioned in the first pages about Cape Alava. A couple of other noted homesteads in the Olympics, still

Humes Ranch on the Elwha River, Olympic Peninsula. (Opposite) Lars Ahlstrom, who lived for 58 years as the "farthest west resident of the continental United States." Also shown, a deserted ranch near Maryhill, Washington.

reached only by trail, are the Humes ranch up the Elwa a couple of miles from Whisky Bend and the Huelsdonk ranch ten miles up the Hoh beyond the ranger station.

This was the summer ranch of the Huelsdonks, who reared a large family and sent the children out to college. After it became part of the national park the cabin deteriorated but the moss-covered orchard still grows. In the early century homesteaders also settled at Taylor Point and at Toleak Point on the wild stretch of seacoast south of La Push.

On the coastal side of the Cascades the jungle reclaims the clearings. In the mountains, cabins collapse under snow. On the arid eastern side, weather-grayed ranch-houses stand for years, slowly sagging as winds whistle through open windows.

Old mines and abandoned camps are often amazing for the size and weight of rusting machinery hauled long distances by wagon or muleback, but those who accomplished the work did it with the dream of riches. They were not there because they loved the soil or the scenery.

The homesteads were created by individual efforts, also heroic in patience and fortitude. The motive was to make an independent living. The stories that go with each place may be unknown to the passerby but he does know that whoever lived there was personally involved 24 hours a day.

Hopes could have ended in despair. Again, though, the homestead could have been quite successful, paying off in satisfactory or even happy years. Then the sadness that goes with old buildings in a wilderness is just a short-term version of the feeling that surrounds the ruined temples of Rome and Egypt. Human generations do not last long.

IN PRAISE OF SPRAY CANS

When the blessings of progress are enumerated, the spray paint-can certainly should be on the list. It makes possible instant archeology. Pictographs now can be inscribed on stone in less than a minute, but will last and last, to be studied by future generations.

It is true the original inhabitants started the rock-writing custom, a genuine example of which is shown here to the left. Having first to manufacture their own pictograph paint, or to chip a petroglyph laboriously into stone, they spent a lot of time in preparing a message. It was no way to put out a bulletin. By the time the reporter finished, readers would ask, "So what's new?"

Consequently the Indians must have saved their efforts for matters they considered to be of importance, perhaps of a religious nature. (The spray-can also delivers religious messages—lower left—without consideration of all the other media available today for that purpose.)

The ancient rock-drawings cannot be translated. Maybe some painted near traditional campsites were little more than doodling for the fun of it. They are still of interest to anthropologists working on the riddles of their symbols and age, and they do furnish clues to the pattern of ancient routes and camps.

In a couple of thousand years archeologists and anthropologists will want to know about us, too. If all our printed, taped and filmed records have disappeared, along with our tin cans, bottles and other litter, think how valuable these modern roadside pictographs will be.

Historians will be able to read the initials of numerous high schools and the years of their graduating classes; advertising messages; popular obscenities of the age, and the names or initials of passersby who were smart enough artist-technicians that they knew how to press the button on a spray-can.

But one of His followers didn't.

Like hundreds of others, these name-writers tried to immortalize themselves with graffiti. This is near George, Washington, a town named for a man who earned his recognition by somewhat more solid accomplishments.

SUPPLEMENTARY READING
FOR SPECIAL INTERESTS

Books are written with the aid of other books. Guidebooks began with the notes of the first travelers in an area and by now they are accretions. Writers gather the latest information and rewrap the package.

When it comes to reference sources, more often than not it is impossible to distinguish between what was looked up for this project —perhaps just to check on a date—and what was absorbed in the past. We originally went to all these places because we already had read or heard about them. That is how tourism began and how it will continue, maybe to the moon.

Advance knowledge about a place or a subject can be the difference between just passing by and genuine enjoyment of it. With that in mind, our "bibliography" is some suggested reading for those who visit the places shown here. We may not have read or referred to a mentioned book, but do know it by reputation.

Many interests can be involved other than sightseeing. The subjects in this book roam through history, geology, archeology, anthropology, botany, wildlife, beachcombing and a lot of hobbies. That is too wide a field to cover as "experts" and we assume that anyone who has made a study of a particular subject could well have served as one of our references on it.

Using ghost towns as an example, the purpose has been to point out that they exist, and as we also pointed out, Lambert Florin is the writer who has specialized in them. Within the region covered here, his books to consult are "Montana-Idaho-Wyoming," "Oregon," "Washington," and "Guide to Western Ghost Towns." He wrote "Historic Western Churches," too. All these are put out by Superior Publishing Co., as is "Old Forts of the Northwest" by Herbert M. Hart.

If shipwrecks are the reader's bag, the general subject is discussed in this book. However, another Superior book is "Disaster Log of Ships" by Jim Gibbs. Gibbs also did "Shipwrecks of the Pacific Coast" for Binfords & Mort.

Two books that help the beachcomber are Ruth Kirk's "The Olympic Seashore" and The Mountaineers' "Trips and Trails, 1" which takes in the north end of the Pacific Ocean front in its final chapters. It is by E. M. Sterling. Either of these pick up the details from where we leave off.

A couple of books designed for hikers and sideroad explorations, both published by The Mountaineers, are "Trips and Trails, 2," also by E. M. Sterling (the Cascades south from Mount Rainier to the Columbia) and "Footloose Around Puget Sound" by Janice Krenmayr. She concentrates on walks of half an hour to most of a day, along beaches, through parks and to lookout points. Maps in these books get down to pinpoint details.

Along that line, a specialty guide is "Beachcombing for Japanese Glass Floats," by Amos L. Wood, which includes trademarks to look for. Other examples of focus on a special subject are "Central Oregon Rock Guide" put out by the U.S. Forest Service and the Bureau of Land Management, and "Covered Bridges of the West" (Washington, Oregon and California) by Kramer A. Adams.

We have taken for granted that rockhounds, birdwatchers, marine life hobbyists and amateur geologists have their own sources of information. On the archeology front, Ruth Kirk told the story of Marmes Man in "The Oldest Man in America," published by Harcourt Brace.

Probably inspired by the success of the Seattle Mountaineers and their books, Don and Roberta Lowe put out "100 Oregon Hiking Trails." It will lead you on into the Columbia waterfalls trails and to the craters in the McKenzie Pass area.

On the history end, the reference books are abundant, from the most general to the most specific. To tune into Harney County (Steens Mountains, Malheur and the cattle barons' story) read "Harney County and Its Range Land" by George Francis Barlow, or "Cattle Country of Peter French" by Giles French (no relation). Both are in libraries.

For almost all eastern Oregon geological and archeological history, a good source is "East of the Cascades" by Phil F. Brogan, a Bend newspaperman who has become almost legendary for his knowledge of the region.

Dick Dunlop wrote "Great Trails of the West," and in gathering the material for it, he and his family actually traveled the routes from beginning to end, as they are today. Four of his stories having to do with the Pacific Northwest are the Mullan Road and Barlow Pass (both here) and the Oregon Trail and the Applegate Road up through southern Oregon.

Al and Jane Salisbury produced long-lasting guidebooks to Western history in "Here Rolled the Covered Wagons" and "Two Captains West."

Historic homes and architecture have been covered by Lucille McDonald in two books, with the help of photographer Werner Lenggenhager. "Where the Washingtonians Lived" and "The Book of Old Time Washington," published by Superior, include such places as Port Townsend, a living museum among cities.

While Superior in Seattle has gained a reputation for showing in photographs how things looked (or look now), the Portland firm of Binfords & Mort has concentrated on publishing new books about Oregon history and on keeping old classics, such as Nard Jones' novel, "Swift Flows the River," in print after Eastern publishers discontinue them. Binfords & Mort issued the Brogan book.

There are other helpful guides. Ralph Friedman published his own book, "Oregon for the Curious," and sold thousands of them as paperbacks. Ralph was a shun-piker for sure and his book is devoted mainly to backroads.

A small booklet was prepared by the "Christmas Valley Women's Club." It is called "Where the Pavement Ends." It costs $1 for 36 pages, but the ladies really did cover the region's attractions very competently.

While the material put out by city and county chambers of commerce must be threshed and gleaned to arrive at the grain in it, instructive information can be obtained by stopping at tourist offices. Some, of course, are more imaginative than others in recognizing a variety of interests among travelers.

As examples, Lane County, Oregon (Eugene is the county seat) has a detailed map with a great deal of information. It is coded to point out every park and camping site and also the covered bridges. Lake County (county seat, Lakeview) has a small pamphlet with a good map.

State tourist departments generally have specialized pamphlets, such as for rockhounds. In Oregon the address is Travel Information Division, Oregon State Highway Department, 101 State Highway Bldg., Salem 97310. Washington's is Tourist Promotion Division, Department of Commerce & Economic Development, General Administration Bldg., Olympia 98501. Address Idaho the same way, at Room 108 State Capitol Bldg., Boise 83707.